ISRAEL'S ENDURING PREDICAMENT

ISRAEL'S ENDURING PREDICAMENT

The Roads That Lead Nowhere

GEW INTELLIGENCE UNIT
Hichem Karoui (Editor)

Global East-West For Studies and Publishing

Copyright © 2023 by GEW Intelligence Unit
(The Voice of The Mediterranean).
Collection: Geopolitics. Editor: Hichem Karoui.
Global East-West LTD

All rights reserved. No part of this book may be reproduced in any manner whatsoever without written permission except in the case of brief quotations embodied in critical articles and reviews.

First Printing, 2023

CONTENTS

Epigraphs	viii
PREFACE	1
INTRODUCTION	5
1 The Palestinian Perspective	18
2 Exploration of the Palestinian Struggle For Survival and Self-Determination	22
3 Examination of the Importance of Land and Religion to the Palestinians	27
4 Discussion on the Significance of Al-Aqsa Mosque in Jerusalem	31
5 Israeli Military Dominance	35
6 Analysis of Israel's Military and Technological Capabilities	39
7 Examination of Previous Military Operations and Their Outcomes	44
8 The Impact of International Support On Israeli Military Capabilities	52
9 The Role of International Community	57

10	Assessment of the Involvement and Influence of Various States and Organisations	63
11	Examination of the Challenges Faced by Palestinians in Gaining International Support	68
12	Analysing the Limitations and Impact of International Resolutions	74
13	Psychological Warfare and Propaganda	79
14	Exploration of the Information War in the Israeli-Palestinian Conflict	85
15	Analysis of Media Coverage and its Impact on Public Perceptions	93
16	Discussion on The Use of Psychological Tactics By Both Sides	99
17	The Role of Arab Governments	105
18	Evaluation of the Impact of Arab Support or Lack Thereof on Palestinian Aspirations	110
19	Discussion on the Challenges Faced by Arab Governments in Supporting the Palestinians	115
20	The Global Muslim Response	121
21	Analysis of the Support Received by Palestinians From the Muslim Population Worldwide	126
22	Examination of the Political, Social, and Economic Dimensions of Muslim Support	131
23	Evaluation of the Potential Consequences For Israel in a Broader Global Context	137
24	Attempts at Peace and Their Failures	145

25	Overview of Previous Peace Initiatives and Negotiations	150
26	Exploration of the Obstacles and Failures in Achieving a Lasting Peace	157
27	Analysis of the Impact of Failed Peace Attempts on the Conflict Dynamics	162
28	The Humanitarian Crisis	169
29	In-depth Analysis of the Humanitarian Situation in Gaza and the West Bank	177
30	Exploration of the Impact of Israeli Policies on Palestinian Living Conditions	182
31	Examination of the Role of International Humanitarian Organisations	187
32	The Way Forward	192
33	Assessment of Potential Pathways Towards a Just and Lasting Peace	197
34	Exploration of Alternative Solutions to the Israeli-Palestinian Conflict	202
35	Discussion on the Importance of International Pressure and Engagement	210
36	Conclusion	218
37	Recapitulation of Key Arguments Presented Throughout the Book	222
38	Call to Action For a Fair Resolution to the Israeli-Palestinian Conflict	228
39	Final Thoughts on the Future of the Region	233

EPIGRAPHS

"Then said Jesus unto him, Put up again thy sword into his place: for all they that take the sword shall perish with the sword."

Peace cannot be achieved through force; it can only be attained through understanding and mutual respect. (Albert Einstein)

The real and lasting victories are those of peace, and not of war. (Ralph Waldo Emerson)

Preface

The Israeli-Palestinian conflict stands as a protracted and multi-layered struggle deeply rooted in historical grievances, political aspirations, and competing claims to land, resources, and sovereignty. This book aims to comprehensively analyse the complexities that have shaped the conflict's current state and explore the deeper dynamics at play.

1.1 Historical Context

To truly grasp the Israeli-Palestinian conflict, it is crucial to delve into its historical backdrop. The origins of this conflict can be traced back to the late 19th century when Zionism emerged as a national movement advocating for the establishment of a Jewish homeland in Palestine. The Balfour Declaration in 1917 by the British Empire, expressing support for such a homeland, further intensified tensions between Jewish immigrants and the native Arab population.

The subsequent years witnessed waves of Jewish immigration to Palestine, with the Jewish population rising significantly. The establishment of Israel as an independent state in 1948 marked a turning point. However, this event, known as the Nakba ("catastrophe" in Arabic), resulted in the displacement and dispossession of hundreds of thousands of Palestinians, deepening their sense of grievance and desire for return.

1.2 Palestinian Perspective: Land and Identity

For the Palestinians, the conflict represents not only a struggle for survival and self-determination but also an endeavour to preserve their national identity. The land holds immense significance, serving as a physical home and a symbol of historical and cultural heritage. Palestinians dream of an independent state with East Jerusalem as its capital, viewing it as a central element of their collective aspirations.

A profound connection to the land has shaped the Palestinian narrative, the historical loss experienced during the Nakba, and ongoing challenges to their identity through settlement expansion, land confiscation, and restrictions on movement. The longing for the right of return for Palestinian refugees, enshrined in UN General Assembly Resolution 194, represents a deeply ingrained quest for justice and restoration.

1.3 Israel's Military Dominance

Israel's military superiority has been a defining characteristic of the conflict. Over the years, it has developed advanced military capabilities backed by substantial defence spending and close alliances with powerful nations. Its technological innovation, intelligence prowess, and well-trained armed forces have allowed it to maintain its military edge.

This military dominance has enabled Israel to launch several military operations in an attempt to secure its borders and protect its population. Yet, despite these interventions, it has not resulted in a definitive solution. The asymmetry of power has created an environment where Israel's military actions have often been met with resistance, escalating grievances among Palestinians and fuelling radicalisation.

1.4 Role of the International Community

The Israeli-Palestinian conflict has attracted significant international attention, with states and organisations attempting to influence the situation in various ways. The international community has provided financial assistance, facilitated negotiations, and sought to mediate peace agreements. However, the international community's lack of a consistent and cohesive approach, often influenced by geopolitical interests, has hindered a sustainable resolution to the conflict.

The engagement of the United States, traditionally a staunch ally of Israel, has further complicated the peace process, as its role has skewed the balance of power and hindered impartiality. The influence and involvement of other regional and international powers, such as Russia, the European Union, and Arab states, have also played a critical role.

1.5 Psychological Warfare and Propaganda

Psychological warfare and propaganda techniques have been employed by both sides to shape public opinion and manipulate narratives. In the digital age, the strategic use of media and social media platforms has become even more significant in influencing perceptions and swaying public support. The battle for legitimacy and the struggle to win hearts and minds play a central role in shaping the trajectory of the conflict.

Israel's military might, while undeniably considerable, face limitations in achieving an enduring victory due to these intricate dynamics. The unwavering determination and resilience of the Palestinian people, coupled with their profound aspirations for self-determination and justice, highlight that a military solution alone cannot extinguish the desire for an independent Palestinian state.

The subsequent chapters will delve further into each of these dimensions, exploring the historical context, the Palestinian perspective, Israel's military dominance, the role of the international community, and the impact of psychological warfare. By thoroughly examining these elements, we can profoundly understand why Israel cannot secure a lasting victory in this complex conflict and explore potential pathways towards a just and sustainable peace.

Introduction

The Israeli-Palestinian conflict is a deeply entrenched and multifaceted issue with significant historical, religious, and political dimensions. It is a clash between two national movements, each with its own narrative, and has been shaped by a myriad of factors over the course of many decades. This extended chapter will delve even further into the complexities of the conflict, providing a comprehensive analysis of key historical events, regional dynamics, and international influences.

The origins of the Israeli-Palestinian conflict can be traced back to the late 19th and early 20th centuries when competing nationalist aspirations emerged among the Jewish and Palestinian Arab populations in Palestine. The Zionist movement, which sought to establish a Jewish homeland in Palestine, gained momentum in the wake of widespread anti-Semitism and the desire for self-determination. However, the growing Jewish presence in Palestine raised concerns among the native Palestinian Arab population, who feared the loss of their own national identity and land.

Tensions between Jews and Arabs escalated further with the British Mandate for Palestine, established after World War I. The Balfour Declaration of 1917, in which Britain expressed support for the establishment of a Jewish homeland, stirred resentment and resistance among the Palestinians. Both communities engaged in acts of violence and protests to assert their claims to the land.

The United Nations partition plan of 1947 was a significant moment in the conflict's history. The proposal aimed to divide Palestine into separate Jewish and Arab states, with Jerusalem placed under international administration. While the Jewish leadership accepted the plan, the Arab states and Palestinians rejected it, viewing it as an unjust division of their homeland. The ensuing 1948 Arab-Israeli war resulted in the creation of the State of Israel and the displacement of hundreds of thousands of Palestinians, a defining moment known as the Nakba, or "catastrophe."

Gaza, a narrow coastal strip with a high population density, and the West Bank, including East Jerusalem, emerged as two territories highly contested between Israelis and Palestinians. Under Israeli control since the 1967 Six-Day War, they have become flashpoints in the conflict.

The 2005 disengagement from Gaza was a significant event that shaped the dynamics of the conflict. Israel unilaterally withdrew its settlers and military forces from the Gaza Strip, intending to improve its security while disentangling itself from the responsibility of governing over a densely populated Palestinian territory. However, the disengagement resulted in the strengthening of Hamas, an Islamist group that ultimately assumed control of Gaza and clashed with Israel in subsequent years. The Israeli blockade of Gaza, imposed in 2007 after Hamas's takeover, further exacerbated the humanitarian crisis in the region, with limited access to essential resources and rampant unemployment.

The West Bank, on the other hand, witnessed the expansion of Israeli settlements, leading to the fragmentation of Palestinian territories and a significant obstacle to the establishment of a viable, contiguous Palestinian state. The Oslo Accords of the 1990s aimed to pave the way for a negotiated solution, with the creation of the Palestinian Authority and the division of the West Bank into areas under Palestinian control (Area A), joint control (Area B), and Israeli control (Area C). However, the failure to halt the expansion of settlements and the continued presence of Israeli military checkpoints and barriers have severely hindered the prospects for Palestinian statehood.

International involvement in the Israeli-Palestinian conflict has been an ongoing issue. Numerous peace initiatives and negotiations have been attempted throughout the years, led by the United States and other international actors. The Camp David Accords in 1978, the Oslo Accords in the 1990s, and the more recent peace proposals such as the Roadmap for Peace and the Arab Peace Initiative all sought to find a mutually acceptable solution for both sides. However, more political will and trust and significant gaps on key issues such as the status of Jerusalem, borders, and the right of return for Palestinian refugees have helped progress.

The regional context in which the Israeli-Palestinian conflict unfolds is crucial to understanding its complexities. Arab governments and states have had varying positions and levels of involvement. Some countries, such as Egypt and Jordan, have engaged in peace initiatives and established diplomatic relations with Israel. However, others, particularly non-Arab Muslim states, have taken a more confrontational stance, viewing the conflict not only through the lens of Palestinian self-determination but also as a broader struggle for the defence of Muslim rights and the Arab world's honour.

The global Muslim response to the Israeli-Palestinian conflict has been influential and impactful. The situation in Gaza and the West Bank resonates deeply with Muslims worldwide, evoking a sense of solidarity and mobilisation. This response is not limited to governments but extends to grassroots movements, civil society organisations, and individuals actively advocating for Palestinians' rights. It is essential to note the diversity of views within the Muslim community, ranging from peaceful advocacy to more extreme and radical positions that play a role in shaping discourse and actions.

The media is critical in shaping public perceptions and understanding of the Israeli-Palestinian conflict. The coverage of events in the region, often influenced by media bias and political agendas, significantly impacts how the conflict is viewed by audiences worldwide. This, in turn, affects public opinion, political support, and the dynamics of international involvement. The explosion of social media platforms has further amplified the voices and narratives in the conflict, allowing direct interaction and the spread of information and misinformation at an unprecedented scale. Psychological warfare, propaganda, and the use of imagery also play a part in shaping the narratives and mobilising support for both Israelis and Palestinians.

Humanitarian considerations are at the heart of the Israeli-Palestinian conflict. The population living in Gaza and the West Bank, particularly in Gaza, has faced immense challenges due to the conflict and its repercussions. Restricted access to essential resources, including clean water, electricity, and healthcare, as well as high levels of poverty and unemployment, have created a dire humanitarian situation. International humanitarian organisations such as the United Nations Relief and Works Agency for Palestine Refugees (UNRWA) play a vital role in providing assistance and relief to Palestinians in need amidst ongoing hostilities.

In conclusion, the Israeli-Palestinian conflict is a profoundly complex issue that involves a range of historical, regional, and international dynamics. Key historical events, such as the partition plan and the Nakba, have shaped the conflict and left deep scars on both Israeli and Palestinian societies. The expansion of settlements, the blockade of Gaza, and the fragmented nature of the West Bank continue to pose significant obstacles to a just and lasting resolution. Effective and inclusive diplomacy, rooted in recognising the rights and aspirations of both Israelis and Palestinians, is essential for sustainable peace. Addressing the underlying grievances, ensuring equal rights and opportunities for all, and fostering a culture of coexistence and understanding are vital steps towards a just resolution of the Israeli-Palestinian conflict.

Historical Background of the Israeli-Palestinian Conflict

The Israeli-Palestinian conflict originated in the late 19th and early 20th centuries as Jewish and Arab nationalist movements emerged in response to the decline of the Ottoman Empire. The British administration's policies both facilitated and hindered Jewish immigration, resulting in a rise in Jewish settlements, particularly during the interwar period. As Jewish immigration continued, Arab opposition grew due to fears of a Jewish majority and the loss of Arab land.

Arab political organisations started to form, with figures like Haj Amin al-Husseini emerging as prominent leaders of Palestinian Arab nationalism. They were concerned that the increasing Jewish presence would lead to the displacement or marginalisation of the Arab population. The Arab revolt against British authorities and Jewish immigration from 1936 to 1939 marked a significant event. Led by Palestinian nationalist leaders, the revolt represented Arab frustration and opposition to British policies and their desire to assert Palestinian Arab national aspirations. However, the revolt was met with a harsh British crackdown, a turning point in the Middle East's relationship with Britain.

Influenced by the fall of the Ottoman Empire, Arab intellectuals and leaders began advocating for an Arab homeland that included Palestine as part of a broader Arab state. They emphasised the Arab identity of Palestine, highlighting its historical and cultural connection to the Arab world. The Balfour Declaration of 1917, written by British Foreign Secretary Arthur Balfour, further heightened tensions. This declaration supported the establishment of a "national home for the Jewish people" in Palestine. While the Zionist movement viewed it as a positive development, the Arab population considered it a betrayal of their national aspirations and right to self-determination, resulting in resistance and outrage.

After World War I, the League of Nations granted Britain a mandate over Palestine, entrusting it with the responsibility to govern and shape its future. The Israeli-Palestinian conflict has deep historical roots, stemming from ideological and nationalist movements among Jews and Arabs in response to the crumbling Ottoman Empire. The Zionist movement, led by Theodor Herzl, sought to establish a Jewish homeland in Palestine, gaining momentum as Jews faced discrimination and persecution in Europe, particularly with the rise of anti-Semitism and the events of the Holocaust. Arab nationalism also gained strength as part of the broader wave of nationalism.

Understanding this historical background is crucial to comprehend the complexity and depth of the Israeli-Palestinian conflict, shaped by deeply ingrained narratives and identities on both sides. However, reaching a just and comprehensive solution requires moving beyond historical analysis and addressing both parties' specific grievances, aspirations, and needs. It necessitates political will, dialogue, compromise, and international involvement to achieve a lasting resolution that tackles the root causes of the conflict, ensuring a peaceful coexistence for Israelis and Palestinians.

Please note that this section provides a more detailed overview of the historical background of the Israeli-Palestinian conflict, covering key events, movements, and dynamics. Exploring additional resources that delve deeper into specific historical periods and perspectives is recommended for a comprehensive understanding.

The conflict, often referred to as the War of Independence or the Nakba (meaning "catastrophe" in Arabic), resulted in a massive displacement and dispossession of Palestinian Arabs. Hundreds of thousands became refugees in neighbouring Arab countries or Israeli-controlled territories, leading to an ongoing refugee crisis. Subsequent conflicts, such as the Six-Day War in 1967 and the Yom Kippur War in 1973, further exacerbated the conflict and expanded Israel's control over Palestinian territories, including the West Bank, Gaza Strip, and East Jerusalem. These territories, initially intended for a future Palestinian state, according to the United Nations proposed partition plan, have since become contentious focal points.

The Israeli-Palestinian conflict encompasses a variety of complex issues, including land and borders, Israeli settlements, security concerns, water rights, and the status of Jerusalem. Many individuals and groups assert historical and religious connections to the land, reinforcing the deep-rooted divisions and animosity. The Holocaust during World War II had a profound impact on the conflict, as the immense loss of Jewish lives at the hands of the Nazis fuelled the urgency for a Jewish homeland and garnered increased international sympathy and support for the Zionist cause.

In 1947, the United Nations proposed a partition plan for Palestine, suggesting the creation of separate Jewish and Arab states with Jerusalem under international administration. While the Jewish leadership accepted the plan, as it recognised their aspirations for statehood, the Arab states and Palestinian Arabs rejected it. They argued that the partition plan unjustly favoured the Jewish population and violated the principle of self-determination. The rejection of the partition plan set the stage for the 1947-1949 war between the newly established state of Israel and the neighbouring Arab states.

Gaza and the West Bank: Overview

The living conditions in Gaza and the West Bank are challenging, with limited access to clean water, electricity, and adequate healthcare.

The Israeli blockade, which has been in place for fifteen years, significantly restricts the flow of goods and stifles the economy. The high population density and unemployment rates, coupled with a lack of economic opportunities, worsen the overall sense of hopelessness and frustration among the people in Gaza. In the West Bank, Palestinians also face limited access to essential services like education and healthcare. The construction and expansion of Israeli settlements, along with restrictions on movement and access to resources, disrupt the lives of Palestinians and create additional humanitarian challenges.

One major obstacle to peace is the ongoing expansion of Israeli settlements in the West Bank. These settlements are considered illegal under international law. They not only undermine the possibility of a viable and contiguous Palestinian state but also impact the daily lives of Palestinians and contribute to internal political rivalries. This division hampers efforts towards unity and coordinated negotiations with Israel.

Security is of utmost importance for both Israelis and Palestinians. Israel argues that strict control over its borders is necessary to protect its citizens from acts of terrorism, citing threats from Hamas and other militant groups. Palestinians, on the other hand, argue that their struggle for freedom and self-determination is often unfairly associated with violence, leading to heavy restrictions and collective punishment. The Israeli military presence in the West Bank, including checkpoints, roadblocks, and the separation barrier, significantly affects freedom of movement, access to services, and economic development. Both sides must address these concerns for sustainable peace.

The people of Gaza and the West Bank face severe humanitarian challenges every day. In Gaza, over two million Palestinians endure difficult living conditions. The political landscape in the region is fragmented and divided among Palestinians. In the West Bank, the Palestinian Authority has limited control due to Israeli military occupation. Israeli settlements and the separation barrier contribute to a fragmented territorial landscape. Criticism is directed towards the Palestinian Authority for its perceived lack of progress in achieving statehood and its handling of internal governance and security. In Gaza, under the control of Hamas since 2007, a humanitarian crisis has unfolded due to the Israeli blockade. The involvement of non-state actors like Hezbollah and Iran adds another layer of complexity. These external factors can either facilitate or hinder the prospects of a sustainable resolution, depending on their alignment of interests and priorities.

The current situation in Gaza and the West Bank is a result of complex and deeply entrenched challenges that impede progress towards a sustainable solution to the Israeli-Palestinian conflict. Divisions among Palestinians, security concerns, the humanitarian crisis in Gaza, settlement expansion, as well as international perspectives and external factors all contribute to the complexities of the conflict. A comprehensive understanding of these dynamics and a genuine commitment from all parties involved are vital for any meaningful attempt at achieving lasting peace. The road to peace requires political will, compromise, and concerted efforts from Israelis, Palestinians, and regional and international stakeholders.

Achieving a lasting peace remains challenging due to divergent interpretations of previous agreements, differing geopolitical interests, and limited progress in direct negotiations between Israelis and Palestinians. The role of external actors and their influence on the peace process is a critical aspect that often requires delicate diplomacy and negotiations. Regional and international dynamics influence the Israeli-Palestinian conflict, further complicating the situation on the ground. Power struggles in the region, the influence of neighbouring countries like Egypt and Jordan, and the interests of global powers such as the United States all contribute to the complex environment in which negotiations occur. Recent regional conflicts and the normalisation of relations between Israel and certain Arab states have the potential to impact the Israeli-Palestinian peace process. Additionally, the continuous construction and expansion of settlements result in the displacement of Palestinian communities, land confiscation, and limited access to resources, water, and education. The international community consistently raises concerns about this issue, urging the Israeli government to halt settlement activities and adhere to international law.

Various international actors have shown interest in the Israeli-Palestinian conflict. The United Nations, the European Union, the United States, as well as individual states have expressed support for a two-state solution, with Israel and Palestine coexisting peacefully and securely. The United Nations, in particular, has passed resolutions and initiatives aimed at addressing the conflict and calling for an end to Israeli occupation. However, reaching a consensus on the necessary steps towards this solution remains challenging due to differing perspectives.

Purpose and scope of the book

The primary purpose of this book is to present a balanced and objective assessment of the Israeli-Palestinian conflict. By doing so, we aim to illuminate the experiences, aspirations and challenges both Israelis and Palestinians face. This conflict has deep roots in history, stemming from competing national aspirations and conflicting claims to land and sovereignty. Through this book, we endeavour to shed light on these complex dynamics, allowing readers to engage with the multifaceted issues at hand.

To achieve this aim, we will critically examine various factors that have contributed to the perpetuation of the conflict. One crucial aspect we address is the military dominance of Israel, which has significantly influenced the power dynamics between the two parties. We explore the implications of this power imbalance, such as the impact on Palestinians' daily lives, their ability to access essential services, and the restrictions on their movement and opportunities for economic development.

By understanding the structural asymmetry, we can better comprehend Palestinians' challenges and barriers to achieving lasting peace.

Additionally, this book seeks to scrutinise the international community's role in facilitating or hindering the resolution of the conflict. Over the years, numerous initiatives, peace plans, and diplomatic efforts have been put forward, often with varying degrees of success. Through a comprehensive analysis, we aim to assess the effectiveness of these international interventions and explore their limitations. We also delve into regional actors' role and influence on the conflict, recognising the significance of external dynamics and forces in shaping the Israeli-Palestinian landscape.

The Scope

While recognising that the Israeli-Palestinian conflict extends beyond the territories of Gaza and the West Bank, this book focuses its analysis on these regions due to their prominence and the significant challenges faced by Palestinians living there. Through an exploration of Gaza, we aim to shed light on the ongoing humanitarian crisis experienced by its residents. The impact of the Israeli blockade, dating back to 2007, has severely constrained the movement of people and goods in and out of Gaza, exacerbating the socio-economic conditions in the region. By examining the lived experiences of Gazans, the book aims to raise awareness and foster empathy towards their plight.

Similarly, by focusing on the West Bank, we aim to unravel the complexities of the Israeli occupation and the daily realities faced by Palestinians living under its jurisdiction. The establishment of Israeli settlements, considered illegal under international law, has dramatically impacted Palestinian land rights, natural resources, and the ability to develop a contiguous and viable state. Through an analysis of the Israeli military presence, checkpoints, and the separation barrier, we seek to illuminate the barriers to Palestinian self-determination and the erosion of their human rights.

Moreover, the book contextualises the Israeli-Palestinian conflict within its broader historical framework. It explores the events that have shaped the conflict, including the 1948 Arab-Israeli war, which led to the displacement of hundreds of thousands of Palestinians, known as the Nakba, meaning "catastrophe." The subsequent creation of the state of Israel and the competing narratives surrounding this event are crucial in understanding the complexities and deep-seated grievances that continue to fuel the conflict to this day.

Furthermore, we examine the impact of subsequent wars, such as the Six-Day War in 1967, which resulted in Israel's occupation of the West Bank, Gaza, and East Jerusalem. We analyse the consequences of this occupation, including the construction of settlements and the entrenchment of Israeli control over crucial areas, raising critical questions about the viability of a two-state solution and the prospects for achieving lasting peace.

Maintaining a Professional Tone

Throughout this book, we maintain a professional and objective tone. We understand this topic's sensitivities and the emotional investment associated with the Israeli-Palestinian conflict. Consequently, we respectfully approach the subject matter and aim to stimulate constructive dialogue. We rely on facts, scholarly analysis, and reputable sources to substantiate our arguments, presenting a range of perspectives while critically evaluating their merits.

Conclusion

This introduction has further elucidated the purpose and scope of this book, focusing on the Israeli-Palestinian conflict, specifically in Gaza and the West Bank. By delving into the historical context, current realities, and potential future scenarios, we strive to deepen the reader's understanding of the multifaceted challenges and possible pathways towards a just and lasting peace. The book's objective analysis aims to contribute to informed discussions and promote positive change surrounding the Israeli-Palestinian conflict.

CHAPTER 1

The Palestinian Perspective

The Israeli-Palestinian conflict is deeply rooted in historical and territorial disputes, which have significantly shaped the Palestinian perspective. In this chapter, we will delve into the Palestinian struggle for survival and self-determination, exploring the importance of land and religion to the Palestinians and shedding light on their perspective as an integral part of understanding the dynamics of the conflict.

Historical Struggles: To understand the Palestinian viewpoint, it is essential to recognise the long-standing hardships faced by the Palestinian people. Palestinians have a rich history rooted in ancient times and have strong connections to the region. Archaeological evidence confirms continuous habitation in the land, and writings from the Bible and ancient Greek and Roman sources mention Palestinian cities and peoples. For many Palestinians, the conflict represents an ongoing struggle to preserve their heritage, protect their ancestral land, and safeguard their cultural identity. The Palestinians have experienced numerous attempts at colonisation and control throughout history. During the era of the Ottoman Empire, the Palestinians endured external influences from European powers seeking to establish a foothold in the area. The arrival of Zionist settlers from Europe in the late 19th century added another layer of complexity to the Palestinian struggle, as the Zionist movement sought to create a Jewish homeland in Palestine.

Land and Territory: The issue of land and territory lies at the core of the Palestinian perspective. Palestinians view themselves as the rightful inhabitants of the land encompassing the West Bank, East Jerusalem, and Gaza, which they believe was unjustly taken away from them. The displacement caused by the establishment of Israel in 1948, known as the Nakba or "catastrophe," remains a deeply traumatic event for many Palestinians. The Nakba resulted in the loss of homes, livelihoods, and cultural heritage, leaving a lasting impact on the Palestinian collective memory. The continued expansion of Israeli settlements in the occupied territories further exacerbates the territorial dispute. Palestinians see these settlements as illegal under international law and as an obstacle to the viability of a Palestinian state. The confiscation of Palestinian land, demolition of homes, and restrictions on movement through checkpoints and barriers have resulted in the fragmentation of Palestinian territories, impeding economic development and stifling social cohesion.

Jerusalem and the Religious Significance: Jerusalem holds immense religious significance for Palestinians, especially the Al-Aqsa Mosque and the Haram al-Sharif compound. These holy sites are not only the third holiest in Islam but also hold profound historical and cultural importance for Palestinians. The presence of Israeli settlers in East Jerusalem and their attempts to assert sovereignty over the city heightens tensions and contributes to Palestinian grievances. Access to the holy sites has been a contentious issue, with restrictions imposed by Israeli authorities often causing frustration and resentment among Palestinians. The recurring clashes between Israeli security forces and Palestinian worshippers at the Al-Aqsa Mosque compound further fuel the sense that religious freedom and cultural heritage are being threatened. As a result, Jerusalem is a focal point for Palestinian resistance movements and a symbol of their national aspirations.

Political Institutions and Leadership: The Palestinian perspective encompasses various political institutions and leadership. The Palestinian Liberation Organisation (PLO), led by Yasser Arafat, emerged in the 1960s as the umbrella organisation representing Palestinian aspirations. The PLO's political arm, the Palestinian Authority (PA), was established in 1994 following the Oslo Accords to govern parts of the occupied territories. However, internal divisions and challenges to their legitimacy have often hindered the Palestinian leadership's ability to unify their voice. The Palestinian people have repeatedly desired democratic representation and accountable governance. Many Palestinians feel disillusioned by the lack of progress in achieving independence and internal issues such as corruption within the Palestinian institutions. Nevertheless, the political institutions and leadership are seen by Palestinians as essential components of their struggle for self-determination and statehood.

Desire for Self-Determination: At the heart of the Palestinian perspective lies their unwavering desire for self-determination. Palestinians seek to exercise their right to determine their political, economic, and social future within a recognised and viable state. The aspiration for statehood embodies the Palestinian dream of attaining independence, freedom, and a sense of collective identity. The absence of a sovereign nation contributes to a sense of ongoing oppression and fuels the fight for Palestinian rights. Palestinians feel marginalised and disempowered by the continued Israeli occupation, which includes checkpoints, security barriers, and restrictions on movement. The lack of control over borders, airspace, and natural resources further impedes their ability to shape their destiny. Palestinians are keenly aware of the obstacles impeding the realisation of their aspirations, including internal divisions, external pressures, and diplomatic challenges. Nevertheless, the desire for self-determination remains deeply ingrained and has fostered resilience among the Palestinian population.

Conclusion: Understanding the Palestinian perspective is crucial for comprehending the complexities of the Israeli-Palestinian conflict. Addressing their historical struggles, the significance of land and territory, religious connections, political institutions, and aspirations for self-determination allows for a more comprehensive analysis of the conflict dynamics. By acknowledging the Palestinian perspective, we can foster a more balanced and nuanced approach towards achieving peaceful peace in the region. Respect for Palestinian rights, including the right to self-determination, remains a fundamental prerequisite for any meaningful resolution to the conflict. It is only through recognising and addressing the concerns and aspirations of both Israelis and Palestinians that a path to peaceful coexistence can be forged.

CHAPTER 2

Exploration of the Palestinian Struggle For Survival and Self-Determination

The Palestinian struggle for survival and self-determination has been a challenging journey spanning decades. This chapter explores the historical, political, economic, and social factors that have influenced the Palestinian quest for survival and determination. Through careful analysis, we aim to highlight the difficulties Palestinians face and their unwavering dedication to securing their rights, preserving their cultural heritage, and establishing an independent state.

Historical Context

To understand the Palestinian struggle, we must contextualise it within the broader historical narrative of the region. Palestinians have inhabited the land of Palestine for centuries, building a rich and diverse cultural heritage deeply rooted in their identity. This connection to the landforms the foundation of the Palestinian struggle, as they have continuously asserted their historical ties to Palestine. Throughout history, different empires and rulers have controlled the region, shaping the demographic and political landscape. In the late 19th century, the introduction of Zionist ideology led to the establishment of Jewish settlements, which eventually culminated in the creation of the State of Israel in 1948. The Nakba, or catastrophe, marked a pivotal moment in the Palestinian struggle, resulting in the displacement of hundreds of thousands of Palestinians and the loss of their homes, lands, and livelihoods.

Recognition of Palestinian Identity

Palestinians have persistently fought against attempts to erase or marginalise their identity. Their collective Palestinian identity combines history, language, cuisine, music, and traditions. Despite the challenges faced, Palestinians have sought to assert and preserve their national identity, utilising cultural expressions as forms of resistance and resilience. Literature, art, and music have played significant roles in solidifying the Palestinian narrative and resisting the narrative of erasure. Both contemporary and historical Palestinian literature offers a poignant window into the Palestinian experience through novels, poetry, and memoirs. Renowned authors such as Mahmoud Darwish, Ghassan Kanafani, and Susan Abulhawa have beautifully captured the essence of the struggle, humanising the Palestinian experience and creating bridges between their stories and the wider international consciousness.

The Impact of Occupation

The Israeli occupation of the West Bank, including East Jerusalem, and the blockade on Gaza have had profound consequences on the daily lives of Palestinians. The construction and expansion of Israeli settlements, the barrier wall, and military checkpoints have created a fragmented and divided Palestinian territory, severely limiting the freedom of movement, access to resources, and economic opportunities. Palestinians have endured systemic discrimination and human rights abuses, ranging from arbitrary arrests and detentions to the demolition of homes and confiscation of land. The psychological impact of occupation, including constant surveillance and the loss of control over one's destiny, cannot be underestimated. Post-traumatic stress disorder, depression, and anxiety affect many Palestinians, particularly children and the youth, who have grown up under these harsh conditions.

Nonviolent Resistance

Palestinians have employed various forms of nonviolent resistance throughout their struggle, inspired by the teachings of Mahatma Gandhi and other leaders of nonviolent movements. Protests, demonstrations, artistic expressions, and civil disobedience have been utilised to confront the occupation, challenge the status quo, and shed light on the injustices faced by Palestinians. The resilience displayed by Palestinian farmers, who continue to cultivate their lands despite settler violence and land confiscation, also serves as a form of nonviolent resistance grounded in a deep connection to the land. These acts of resistance showcase the determination of Palestinians to assert their rights, maintain their dignity, and pursue justice through peaceful means.

The Role of International Conventions and Legal Challenges

The international legal framework, including United Nations resolutions and international conventions, has played a critical role in supporting the Palestinian cause for justice and self-determination. Palestinians have sought justice through legal means, employing avenues such as the International Criminal Court (ICC) and other international legal mechanisms to hold accountable those responsible for human rights violations. Despite facing challenges and obstacles, legal actions have provided Palestinians with opportunities to bring attention to their plight, seek justice, and challenge the impunity of those perpetrating crimes against them. The cases brought before international courts highlight the urgency of addressing the occupation and the international community's responsibility to ensure respect for international law.

Diaspora and Refugees

The Palestinian struggle for survival and self-determination extends beyond the territories currently occupied by Israel. The Palestinian diaspora, consisting of millions of Palestinians around the world, exists as a vibrant community upholding their national identity, maintaining connections to their ancestral homeland, and advocating for their rights. Palestinians dispersed across different continents have significantly contributed to various fields of endeavour, including academia, art, science, and politics. Palestinian refugees, numbering in the millions, continue to face challenges in their host countries, often deprived of basic rights and living in precarious conditions. The right of return for Palestinians, a core component of their struggle, remains central to their aspirations for justice and self-determination. The Palestinian Refugee Issue bears a profound humanitarian significance that requires international attention and action to find a just and comprehensive solution.

Conclusion

The Palestinian struggle for survival and self-determination is deeply entrenched in their historical experiences, unyielding collective identity, and steadfast resistance against oppression. The challenges posed by occupation, preserving their cultural heritage, and pursuing justice through legal means continue to shape their journey. The endurance and resilience of the Palestinian people, despite the manifold hardships they have endured, is a testament to their determination and unwavering hope for a better future. International solidarity and support are vital in ensuring that the rights and aspirations of Palestinians are recognised and fulfilled. The path to a just and lasting peace in the region requires genuine efforts to address the root causes of the conflict, uphold international law, and respect the inherent dignity and rights of all individuals, including the Palestinians.

CHAPTER 3

Examination of the Importance of Land and Religion to the Palestinians

The Israeli-Palestinian conflict is deeply rooted in historical and territorial disputes, which have significantly shaped the Palestinian perspective. In this chapter, we will delve into the Palestinian struggle for survival and self-determination, exploring the importance of land and religion to the Palestinians and shedding light on their perspective as an integral part of understanding the dynamics of the conflict.

Historical Struggles: To comprehend the Palestinian perspective, it is crucial to acknowledge the historical struggles endured by the Palestinian people. Palestinians trace their roots back to ancient times and have deep historical ties to the region. Archaeological evidence confirms continuous habitation in the land, and writings from the Bible, as well as ancient Greek and Roman sources, mention Palestinian cities and peoples. For many Palestinians, the conflict represents an ongoing struggle to preserve their heritage, protect their ancestral land, and safeguard their cultural identity. The Palestinians have experienced numerous attempts at colonisation and control throughout history. During the era of the Ottoman Empire, the Palestinians endured external influences from European powers seeking to establish a foothold in the area. The arrival of Zionist settlers from Europe in the late 19th century added another layer of complexity to the Palestinian struggle, as the Zionist movement sought to create a Jewish homeland in Palestine.

Land and Territory: The issue of land and territory lies at the core of the Palestinian perspective. Palestinians view themselves as the rightful inhabitants of the land encompassing the West Bank, East Jerusalem, and Gaza, which they believe was unjustly taken away from them. The displacement caused by the establishment of Israel in 1948, known as the Nakba or "catastrophe," remains a deeply traumatic event for many Palestinians. The Nakba resulted in the loss of homes, livelihoods, and cultural heritage, leaving a lasting impact on the Palestinian collective memory. The continued expansion of Israeli settlements in the occupied territories further exacerbates the territorial dispute. Palestinians see these settlements as illegal under international law and as an obstacle to the viability of a Palestinian state. The confiscation of Palestinian land, demolition of homes, and restrictions on movement through checkpoints and barriers have resulted in the fragmentation of Palestinian territories, impeding economic development and stifling social cohesion.

Jerusalem and the Religious Significance: Jerusalem holds immense religious significance for Palestinians, especially the Al-Aqsa Mosque and the Haram al-Sharif compound. These holy sites are not only the third holiest in Islam but also hold deep historical and cultural importance for Palestinians. The presence of Israeli settlers in East Jerusalem and their attempts to assert sovereignty over the city heightens tensions and contributes to Palestinian grievances. Access to the holy sites has been a contentious issue, with restrictions imposed by Israeli authorities often causing frustration and resentment among

Palestinians. The recurring clashes between Israeli security forces and Palestinian worshippers at the Al-Aqsa Mosque compound further fuel the sense that religious freedom and cultural heritage are being threatened. As a result, Jerusalem is a focal point for Palestinian resistance movements and a symbol of their national aspirations.

Political Institutions and Leadership: The Palestinian perspective encompasses various political institutions and leadership. The Palestinian Liberation Organisation (PLO), led by Yasser Arafat, emerged in the 1960s as the umbrella organisation representing Palestinian aspirations. The PLO's political arm, the Palestinian Authority (PA), was established in 1994 following the Oslo Accords to govern parts of the occupied territories. However, internal divisions and challenges to their legitimacy have often hindered the Palestinian leadership's ability to unify their voice. The Palestinian people have repeatedly desired democratic representation and accountable governance. Many Palestinians feel disillusioned by the lack of progress in achieving independence and internal issues such as corruption within the Palestinian institutions. Nevertheless, the political institutions and leadership are seen by Palestinians as essential components of their struggle for self-determination and statehood.

Desire for Self-Determination: At the heart of the Palestinian perspective lies their unwavering desire for self-determination. Palestinians seek to exercise their right to determine their political, economic, and social future within a recognised and viable state. The aspiration for statehood embodies the Palestinian dream of attaining independence, freedom, and a sense of collective identity. The absence of a sovereign nation contributes to a sense of ongoing oppression and fuels the fight for Palestinian rights. Palestinians feel marginalised and disempowered by the continued Israeli occupation, which includes checkpoints, security barriers, and restrictions on movement. The lack of control over borders, airspace, and natural resources further impedes their ability to shape their own destiny. Palestinians are keenly aware of the obstacles impeding the realisation of their aspirations, including internal divisions, external pressures, and diplomatic challenges. Nevertheless, the desire for self-determination remains deeply ingrained and has fostered resilience among the Palestinian population.

Conclusion: Understanding the Palestinian perspective is crucial for comprehending the complexities of the Israeli-Palestinian conflict. Addressing their historical struggles, the significance of land and territory, religious connections, political institutions, and aspirations for self-determination allows for a more comprehensive analysis of the conflict dynamics. By acknowledging the Palestinian perspective, we can foster a more balanced and nuanced approach towards achieving a peaceful peace in the region. Respect for Palestinian rights, including the right to self-determination, remains a fundamental prerequisite for any meaningful resolution to the conflict. It is only through recognising and addressing the concerns and aspirations of both Israelis and Palestinians that a path to peaceful coexistence can be forged.

CHAPTER 4

Discussion on the Significance of Al-Aqsa Mosque in Jerusalem

The Al-Aqsa Mosque holds immense religious and political significance in the complex and long-standing Israeli-Palestinian conflict. Located in the heart of the Old City of Jerusalem, the mosque complex encompasses the Al-Aqsa Mosque, the iconic Golden Dome of the Rock, and various other structures. It is considered the third holiest site in Islam after the Masjid al-Haram in Mecca and the Prophet's Mosque in Medina.

Religiously, the Al-Aqsa Mosque is cherished by Muslims worldwide as a symbol of faith, history, and unity. According to Islamic tradition, it is believed to be where the Prophet Muhammad embarked on his miraculous Night Journey, during which he ascended through the heavens and encountered various prophets before reaching the divine presence. This celestial journey, known as the Isra and Mi'raj, marks a seminal event in Islamic theology and underscores the spiritual significance of the Al-Aqsa Mosque. In addition, Jerusalem is mentioned in the Quran as the location of the Prophet Muhammad's initial qibla, or direction of prayer, before it was changed to Mecca.

Beyond its religious importance, Al-Aqsa Mosque bears great political weight in the Israeli-Palestinian conflict. Its significance resides not only in the mosque itself but also in its location within the wider Old City, which is divided into several quarters: Muslim, Jewish, Christian, and Armenian. The compound is situated adjacent to the Western Wall, the holiest site in Judaism. This proximity has fuelled centuries of tensions between followers of different faiths and contributed to the struggle for control over Jerusalem.

Historically, control and ownership of Jerusalem, and thus the Al-Aqsa Mosque, have changed hands numerous times. Islamic rule over the city began in 638 CE when the Rashidun Caliphate conquered it from the Byzantine Empire. From then on, the Al-Aqsa Mosque became a focal point of Jerusalem's Islamic administration and religious practice. Over the centuries, the mosque developed as a central site for religious and political activities, attracting pilgrims and intellectuals from across the Islamic world.

The Crusades in the 11th and 12th centuries brought a period of Christian rule in Jerusalem, during which the Al-Aqsa Mosque was converted into a church. However, Muslim rule was restored under Saladin in 1187, and Jerusalem became a Muslim-majority city again. Under the subsequent rule of the Mamluk and Ottoman empires, the Al-Aqsa Mosque complex underwent various expansions and renovations, turning it into the architectural wonder it is today. Each successive Islamic empire contributed to the development and preservation of the holy site, cementing it as a point of pride and identity for the entire Muslim world.

The British Mandate for Palestine, established after World War I, marked a new period of governance over Jerusalem. However, tensions between the Jewish and Arab communities, as well as the struggle for self-determination, intensified, leading to increasing unrest. Following the 1947 UN Partition Plan, Jerusalem was supposed to become an international city administered by the United Nations. However, the subsequent war in 1948 resulted in the division of Jerusalem, with the eastern portion, including the Old City and Al-Aqsa Mosque, coming under Jordanian control.

The 1967 Six-Day War between Israel and the Arab states had a significant impact on the status of Jerusalem and the Al-Aqsa Mosque. Israel's capture of the entire city, including the Old City, marked a turning point in the conflict. Under the Israeli administration, the Islamic Waqf retained religious authority over the compound, while Israel maintained security control. However, successive governments' actions regarding the mosque have been a consistent source of tension between Palestinians and Israelis.

For Palestinians, the Al-Aqsa Mosque represents not only their religious identity but also their national aspirations. It is a powerful symbol of their connection to the land and their struggle for self-determination. Any perceived threats or restrictions on access to the mosque, such as plans for Jewish prayer at the site or the presence of Israeli security forces, have historically sparked widespread outrage and protests. Palestinians fear that their historical and religious ties to Jerusalem are being eroded, amplifying their grievances and fuelling ongoing tensions.

In recent decades, incidents involving the Al-Aqsa Mosque have proven to be pivotal in igniting escalations of violence between Israeli forces and Palestinians. Clashes and outbreaks of violence often begin as a result of perceived affronts to the mosque, such as visits by Israeli politicians or altercations within the compound. These incidents can quickly reverberate throughout the region, triggering wider confrontations and exacerbating the existing deep-seated grievances and political challenges.

Understanding the profound significance of the Al-Aqsa Mosque is crucial for comprehending the complex dynamics in the Israeli-Palestinian conflict. It is not merely a religious structure but also a rallying point for political aspirations, national identity, and historical claims. Its sanctity, symbolism, and contested nature make it an inextricable component of the broader struggle for control over Jerusalem and the urgent need for a just and lasting resolution to the Israeli-Palestinian conflict.

CHAPTER 5

Israeli Military Dominance

Israel's military strength and dominance have played a pivotal role in the Israeli-Palestinian conflict. From its technological advancements and highly trained personnel to its strategic capabilities, Israel's military superiority has been a defining factor in the conflict. This chapter aims to provide a comprehensive analysis, exploring the various facets of Israel's military dominance and its implications within the context of the conflict.

Israel's Military Capabilities

Israel has consistently allocated a significant portion of its GDP towards developing a robust military infrastructure. Its commitment to maintaining a powerful military is rooted in the nation's unique security challenges in the region. This dedicated investment has allowed the country to acquire state-of-the-art weaponry, advanced military technology, and efficient intelligence systems. As a percentage of GDP, the Israeli defence budget consistently ranks among the highest globally, facilitating continuous improvements and modernisation of its defence forces. Israel excels in air defence, cyber warfare, precision airstrikes, and surveillance systems, safeguarding a significant military advantage.

Technological Advancements

Israel's unwavering dedication to innovation and research has propelled its military capabilities forward. The nation's defence industries have made groundbreaking contributions to developing advanced weaponry and military technologies. With a steadfast focus on research and development, Israel has fostered an environment conducive to technological breakthroughs. This commitment has resulted in the creation of cutting-edge defence systems, including missile interceptors, unmanned aerial vehicles (UAVs), and advanced surveillance and intelligence systems. Israel's miniaturisation, drone technology, and artificial intelligence expertise have revolutionised its operational efficiency, enabling precise and effective military strategies. These technological advancements enhance Israel's capabilities and position it as a global leader in defence technology.

Historical Military Operations

Israel's military dominance has been clearly demonstrated through numerous historical military operations. Throughout its existence, Israel has successfully defeated conventional armies and effectively neutralised threats to its security. The 1948 Arab-Israeli War saw the newly established state of Israel fend off attacks from surrounding Arab nations, asserting its territorial integrity. The Six-Day War in 1967 showcased Israel's swift and decisive military capabilities, resulting in the acquisition of additional territories. The Yom Kippur War in 1973 challenged

Israel initially but exhibited the nation's resilience and adaptability as it turned the tide of the conflict. These historical successes have not only solidified Israel's military reputation but have had profound impacts on the balance of power in the region.

International Support

Israel's military dominance has been further reinforced by substantial international support, most notably from the United States. The U.S. has long been a key ally of Israel, providing significant military aid, advanced weaponry, and diplomatic backing. This support has bolstered Israel's military capabilities and elevated its status as a significant regional power. The close relationship between the Israeli and American defence sectors has facilitated extensive cooperation, joint military exercises, and technological exchanges. Beyond the United States, Israel has actively sought to establish military cooperation with other countries, sharing its expertise and engaging in joint military ventures. These collaborative efforts have fostered valuable partnerships, expanding Israel's military network and enhancing its military prowess.

Implications and Challenges

While Israel's military dominance has undoubtedly provided a significant advantage in the conflict, it has also presented unique challenges. The perception of overwhelming military force has fuelled resentment and resistance among Palestinians and other regional actors. The asymmetric nature of the conflict, with Israel possessing advanced military capabilities, has led to concerns about the imbalance of power and potential abuses. Moreover, the disproportionate use of military actions resulting in civilian casualties has drawn international criticism, raising concerns about Israel's commitment to humanitarian values. Consequently, Israel faces the task of balancing its military operations with diplomacy and dialogue to address the underlying issues and aspirations of both Israelis and Palestinians.

Conclusion

Israel's military dominance stands as a critical factor shaping the Israeli-Palestinian conflict. Israel has established a position of strength through its technological advancements, well-trained military personnel, and international support. However, achieving a just and lasting peace requires more than military considerations. It necessitates addressing the root causes of the conflict, confronting the political complexities, and genuinely understanding the aspirations of both Israelis and Palestinians. A comprehensive and sustainable solution can only be achieved through a multifaceted approach encompassing diplomacy, dialogue, compromise, and respect for humanitarian values. While Israel's military dominance may provide short-term security, true security lies in the establishment of a peaceful and equitable coexistence between Israelis and Palestinians.

CHAPTER 6

Analysis of Israel's Military and Technological Capabilities

This chapter will explore Israel's military capabilities and technological advancements that have played a significant role in shaping the dynamics of the Israeli-Palestinian conflict. Israel has made substantial investments in its military infrastructure, making it one of the most technologically advanced armed forces globally. The purpose of this analysis is to offer an objective assessment of Israel's military prowess and its impact on the conflict.

1. Historical Background

To understand Israel's military capabilities, it is crucial to consider the historical context that shaped its defence strategies. The formation of the Israeli state in 1948 under challenging circumstances necessitated the development of a robust military apparatus to ensure its survival in a hostile region. Israel faced numerous wars and conflicts, leading to a continuous focus on military innovation and technological advancements.

2. Technological Superiority

a) Intelligence Gathering: Israel has excelled in intelligence gathering through sophisticated surveillance systems, satellite technology, and a vast network of informants. The Israeli intelligence agencies, such as Mossad and Shin Bet, have consistently demonstrated their ability to obtain crucial information for preemptive measures. They employ advanced technologies that include signal interception, geolocation, and pattern recognition, enabling them to stay proactive in countering security threats. Israel's intelligence capabilities extend to areas like cyber intelligence, where they effectively monitor and counter cyber threats.

b) Air Defence Systems: Israel has developed cutting-edge air defence systems, including the Iron Dome, which has proven highly effective against rocket and missile attacks. The Iron Dome employs radar, tracking systems, and interceptor missiles to detect and intercept incoming projectiles, minimising casualties and damage. Israel's missile defence capabilities are also strengthened by systems like David's Sling, capable of intercepting short-range and medium-range ballistic missiles, and Arrow, designed to counter long-range ballistic missile threats. This multi-layered defence approach has significantly enhanced Israel's strategic capabilities.

c) Cybersecurity: Israel has emerged as a global leader in cybersecurity, with advanced capabilities to fend off cyber threats. Its proficiency in this domain has been instrumental in countering external threats and safeguarding critical infrastructure. Israeli cybersecurity firms offer innovative solutions in areas like threat intelligence, network protection, and incident response. The country's focus on cyber defence has enhanced its military capabilities and contributed to its economic growth through a thriving cybersecurity industry. Israel's cyber capabilities extend beyond defence, as it is known for its offencive cyber operations and capabilities to disrupt adversaries' networks.

d) Military Technology: Israel has significantly invested in military research and development, resulting in groundbreaking technological innovations. It boasts advanced weaponry, including precision-guided missiles, advanced fighter aircraft, unmanned aerial vehicles (UAVs), and sophisticated communication systems. Israel's defence industry has pioneered in developing compact surveillance systems, miniaturised munitions, and fighter jets equipped with state-of-the-art avionics. It also leads in the field of drone technology, with UAVs playing a crucial role in intelligence, surveillance, and targeted strikes. In recent years, Israel has been at the forefront of developing autonomous weapon systems, including armed robots, which could offer significant advantages in future conflicts.

3. *Military Operations and Tactics*

Israel's military operations have demonstrated advanced technological capabilities and effective tactical planning and execution. The Israeli Defence Forces (IDF) have developed comprehensive strategies for quick mobilisation, intelligence-based operations, and asymmetrical warfare. Israel's "combined arms" doctrine emphasises the integration of air, ground, and naval forces to carry out precise and coordinated operations. The IDF's operational approach includes rapid and agile responses, exploiting technological advantages, and leveraging intelligence to disrupt enemy plans. Special forces such as the elite Sayeret units are crucial in intelligence gathering, direct action, and counterterrorism operations. Israel's military operations are known for their emphasis on minimising collateral damage and civilian casualties, utilising precision-strike capabilities and advanced intelligence to mitigate unintended consequences.

4. *International Collaboration*

Israel has actively pursued collaborations with other military powers, such as the United States, in technological research and development. These partnerships, along with advantageous defence agreements, have further enhanced Israel's military capabilities. Key areas of collaboration include intelligence sharing, joint military exercises, and technological exchanges. Israel benefits from its association with the U.S., which provides substantial military aid, advanced technology transfers, and support in areas like missile defence systems. Additionally, Israel has established partnerships with other countries, including Germany, France, and India, facilitating cooperation in defence R&D, training, and military sales. International collaborations also facilitate the expansion of Israel's defence industry, enabling it to export military technology to countries worldwide.

Conclusion

Israel's military capabilities and technological advancements have undeniably played a crucial role in shaping the Israeli-Palestinian conflict. Its commitment to military innovation, intelligence gathering, and preemptive strategies has given Israel a considerable advantage in defending its borders and maintaining military superiority. The country's significant investments in intelligence, air defence systems, cybersecurity, military technology, and international collaborations have yielded impressive results. However, it is crucial to recognise that while military power is essential for safeguarding national security, it should be coupled with diplomatic efforts and meaningful negotiations to achieve a lasting resolution to the Israeli-Palestinian conflict. A comprehensive approach considering political, social, and humanitarian aspects is necessary to achieve sustainable regional peace.

CHAPTER 7

Examination of Previous Military Operations and Their Outcomes

To gain a comprehensive understanding of the Israeli-Palestinian conflict, it is imperative to examine previous military operations conducted by Israel and their outcomes. This chapter aims to provide an in-depth analysis of the historical context and the impact of these operations on the conflict dynamics.

1. Historical Context

To appropriately evaluate the outcomes of previous military operations, it is crucial to consider their historical context. This includes understanding the reasons behind these operations, such as threats to Israeli security, responses to terrorist attacks, or attempts to assert control over territories. By exploring the motivations and circumstances surrounding each operation, we can gain insight into the intentions and objectives of Israel's military actions.

2. Operation Cast Lead (2008-2009)

One significant military operation that warrants examination is Operation Cast Lead. Launched by Israel in response to ongoing rocket attacks from Gaza, this operation aimed to degrade Hamas' infrastructure and military capabilities. It involved extensive air and ground operations, resulting in significant Palestinian casualties and infrastructural damage.

Operation Cast Lead began on December 27, 2008, and lasted approximately three weeks. Israel's stated objective was to halt the rocket attacks on its southern communities, which had become increasingly frequent and threatening. The operation involved heavy bombing campaigns, targeting Hamas' military installations, rocket-launching sites, and infrastructure. In addition to airstrikes, the Israeli Forces also conducted a ground incursion into Gaza.

While Israel claimed that it took measures to minimise civilian casualties and warned residents to evacuate targeted areas, the densely populated nature of Gaza made it challenging to prevent civilian deaths. Human rights organisations, including Amnesty International and Human Rights Watch, accused Israel of using excessive force and not adequately distinguishing between military and civilian targets. These allegations were primarily based on the significant number of civilian casualties, including women, children, and older people.

The operation ended with an Egyptian-brokered ceasefire on January 18, 2009. While Israel declared that it had achieved its objectives of weakening Hamas's capabilities and reducing rocket fire, the operation drew considerable international criticism and condemnation. Many argued that the extensive destruction and loss of civilian lives worsened the already dire humanitarian situation in Gaza and further strained Israeli-Palestinian relations.

Despite the criticism, Operation Cast Lead did have some effects on the Israeli-Palestinian conflict dynamics. It weakened Hamas' military capabilities, disrupted its operational infrastructure, and achieved a temporary reduction in rocket attacks. However, the long-term impact of the operation on the conflict's resolution was limited. The deep-rooted grievances, political tensions, and underlying issues remained unaddressed, contributing to a cycle of violence and subsequent military operations in the years to come.

3. Operation Protective Edge (2014)

Another major operation that shaped the Israeli-Palestinian conflict was Operation Protective Edge. This military campaign was launched by Israel in response to rocket attacks from Gaza and aimed to halt the firing of rockets into Israeli territory. The operation involved airstrikes and ground incursions, resulting in significant Palestinian casualties, infrastructure devastation, and displacement.

Operation Protective Edge began on July 8, 2014, following a steady escalation of hostilities between Israel and Hamas. Hamas had intensified its rocket attacks on Israeli towns and cities, leading Israel to launch a full-scale military operation. The Israeli army's objective was to dismantle Hamas' extensive network of tunnels used for smuggling weapons and infiltrating Israeli territory.

The operation consisted of a broad aerial campaign targeting Hamas infrastructure, rocket launchers, and weapons storage facilities. Additionally, Israel employed ground forces to attack and destroy the tunnels extending from Gaza into Israeli territory. The operation lasted for 50 days, resulting in a high number of casualties, including many civilians.

Human rights organisations raised concerns over the targeting of civilian areas, noting that schools, hospitals, and residential buildings were hit during the campaign. They argued that Israel had disregarded the principle of proportionality and failed to take sufficient precautions to prevent civilian casualties. On the other hand, Israel maintained that it had taken significant measures to minimise civilian harm, attributing civilian deaths to Hamas' use of civilian infrastructure for military purposes.

Operation Protective Edge ceased with an Egypt-brokered ceasefire on August 26, 2014. While Israel claimed success in dealing a significant blow to Hamas' military capabilities and reducing rocket attacks, the operation's immense toll on Palestinians, mainly civilians, drew international concern and condemnation. The extensive destruction of infrastructure, displacement of populations, and long-lasting psychological trauma in Gaza further complicated the prospects for peace.

The aftermath of Operation Protective Edge demonstrated the challenges faced in finding a lasting solution to the conflict. Hamas, despite significant infrastructure damage, managed to rebuild its military capabilities, including tunnel networks and rocket arsenals. The operation did not deter future rocket attacks, and sporadic violence continued to persist, highlighting the underlying issues of the conflict that needed to be addressed beyond military means.

4. *Outcomes and Consequences*

Examining the outcomes of previous military operations is essential in understanding their impact on the Israeli-Palestinian conflict. It is important to note that the consequences are multifaceted and often extend beyond immediate military objectives. While these operations may have temporarily diminished Hamas's capabilities and deterred attacks to some extent, they have also fuelled animosity among the Palestinian population, increased radicalisation, and propelled the cycle of violence.

One of the primary consequences of these operations has been the impact on civilian populations. The heavy toll on Palestinian civilians, including deaths, injuries, and displacement, has eroded trust and further deepened the animosity between the two sides. The extensive destruction of infrastructure, including homes, schools, hospitals, and vital supplies, has also exacerbated the humanitarian crisis in Gaza and hindered prospects for economic development.

Moreover, these military operations have led to a rise in radicalisation and militancy among segments of the Palestinian population. The perceived injustices, loss of lives, and destruction of livelihoods have fuelled anger and frustration, pushing some individuals towards extremist ideologies, including support for Hamas. This radicalisation further complicates efforts to achieve a peaceful resolution and increases the chances of renewed violence.

The consequences of these operations are not limited to the Palestinian side alone. In Israel, the constant threat of rocket attacks and the need to respond militarily have led to heightened anxiety and insecurity among the population, impacting daily life and perpetuating a cycle of violence. Furthermore, the international perception of Israel's conduct during these operations has often been unfavourable, straining diplomatic relations and complicating efforts to achieve a peaceful resolution.

5. *International Perception and Condemnation*

Previous military operations have also garnered international attention and condemnation. Criticism from human rights organisations and the international community at large has centred around issues such as the disproportionate use of force, civilian casualties, and the impact on the humanitarian situation in Gaza and the West Bank.

These criticisms have had both short-term and long-term implications for Israel's international reputation, diplomatic relations, and pursuit of a peaceful resolution to the conflict.

The international community, including the United Nations, has repeatedly called for impartial investigations into alleged violations of international humanitarian law and human rights abuses during these military operations. Resolutions have been put forth in forums like the UN Security Council and the UN Human Rights Council, reflecting concerns over the conduct and consequences of these operations. The international pressure has pushed for greater accountability and efforts to prevent civilian casualties and ensure respect for human rights in future military engagements.

6. *Impact on the Peace Process*

The impact of previous military operations on the Israeli-Palestinian peace process has been significant. These operations have often led to a breakdown in negotiations and a hardening of positions, making it increasingly difficult to find common ground and achieve a lasting resolution.

The use of force and the resulting casualties have deepened mistrust and scepticism between the two sides. Palestinian leaders have accused Israel of using excessive force and undermining the prospects for peace. In contrast, Israeli leaders argue that military operations are necessary for self-defence and deterring further attacks. This fundamental divergence in perspectives has hindered the progress of peace negotiations and perpetuated the cycle of violence.

Furthermore, these military operations have also impacted the internal dynamics within both Israeli and Palestinian society. In Israel, the public's perception of security threats and their desire for a solid response to violence have often shaped political discourse and influenced the direction of policy. In the Palestinian territories, the loss of lives and extensive destruction have bolstered support for Hamas and other militant factions, further undermining the authority of the Palestinian Authority and complicating efforts to reach a unified position for negotiations.

The international community's response to these military operations has also impacted the peace process. The condemnation and criticism from international actors have often led to increased pressure on both sides to resume negotiations and find a peaceful resolution. However, it has also deepened the divide between Israel and the international community, making it more challenging to facilitate impartial mediation and achieve consensus on a way forward.

7. Lessons Learnt

Analysing the outcomes and consequences of previous military operations provides vital lessons for future engagements and efforts towards conflict resolution.

First, there is a need for a balanced approach that upholds the principles of proportionality, necessity, and distinction. Military operations should aim to minimise civilian casualties, protect vital civilian infrastructure, and target only legitimate military targets. Striking the right balance is crucial to avoid exacerbating humanitarian concerns, radicalising populations, and eroding international support.

Second, military operations alone cannot address the underlying causes of the conflict. While short-term military objectives may be achieved, long-lasting peace can only be realised through comprehensive political negotiations and a focus on the root issues, including the status of Jerusalem, Israeli settlements, borders, and the right of return for Palestinian refugees.

Third, the involvement of impartial mediators and the international community is crucial in ensuring accountability and facilitating a peaceful resolution. The international community should proactively mediate negotiations, support humanitarian efforts, and promote de-escalation to prevent further violence.

Lastly, emphasising the importance of dialogue, trust-building, and confidence-building measures can help break the cycle of violence and create an environment conducive to negotiations. This includes encouraging people-to-people exchanges, promoting reconciliation initiatives, and fostering mutual understanding and empathy between Israelis and Palestinians.

Conclusion

Examining previous military operations' historical context, outcomes, and consequences provides critical insights into the Israeli-Palestinian conflict. These military operations have profoundly impacted the conflict dynamics, including the humanitarian situation, the peace process, and international perceptions. Understanding these complexities is essential to inform future approaches towards achieving a just and sustainable resolution to the Israeli-Palestinian conflict.

CHAPTER 8

The Impact of International Support On Israeli Military Capabilities

The Israeli military, renowned for its technological sophistication and operational effectiveness, owes much of its prowess to international support. The support, both overt and covert, from various countries, has significantly influenced Israel's military capabilities and has played a crucial role in shaping its defence infrastructure. This chapter delves deeper into the multifaceted aspects of international support and examines the extent to which it has bolstered Israel's military superiority.

1. *Diplomatic Support*

Israel has long enjoyed strong diplomatic backing, predominantly from the United States. This support has been instrumental in shaping Israel's military capabilities, offering political legitimacy and facilitating access to advanced weaponry. The close alliance with the United States has translated into consistent and extensive military aid, including substantial financial contributions and the provision of modern weapons systems. The qualitative edge provided by these military supplies has enabled Israel to project power in the region and achieve tactical superiority over its adversaries.

Moreover, diplomatic backing has played a crucial role in securing international recognition and legitimacy for Israel's military activities. It has shielded Israel from severe diplomatic repercussions following military operations and enabled it to maintain its actions within a politically favourable environment. This diplomatic cushioning is a strategic asset, preserving Israel's military capabilities and providing a foundation for its defence doctrine.

2. *Technological and Intelligence Cooperation*

Israel's military strength owes much to robust technological collaboration with various international partners, notably the United States. This collaboration has allowed Israel to access cutting-edge military technologies, often developed jointly that has significantly enhanced its capabilities in intelligence gathering, surveillance, precision strikes, and defensive measures. The transfer of advanced weapons, such as fighter jets, missile defence systems, and precision-guided munitions, has propelled Israel's military capabilities to unprecedented levels.

Israel's prowess in intelligence gathering owes much to international cooperation as well. Sharing intelligence with trusted allies, such as the United States, has provided critical information on regional threats and instabilities, enabling preemptive actions and enhancing operational preparedness. Furthermore, joint research and development efforts have facilitated the creation of sophisticated intelligence systems, cyber defence capabilities, and advanced surveillance technologies, positioning Israel as a global leader in these domains.

3. Training and Military Exchanges

International partnerships have played a pivotal role in refining Israel's military capabilities through extensive training programmes and military exchanges. Israeli Defence Forces (IDF) personnel often engage in joint exercises, receive specialised training, and share operational expertise with foreign counterparts. Collaboration with renowned militaries offers a unique opportunity for the IDF to learn from diverse operational experiences, develop innovative tactics, and hone its skills in areas such as counterterrorism, special operations, and urban warfare.

These training programmes foster camaraderie and cooperation among partner nations, strengthening regional security networks. Additionally, military exchanges allow Israel to showcase its technological advancements, share best practices, and enhance its reputation as a valuable partner and contributor to global security.

4. Funding and Economic Support

International financial aid and economic support have played a pivotal role in Israel's military capabilities. The continued support from the United States and other strategic partners has enabled Israel to invest heavily in defence research and development. Financial resources facilitate the acquisition of advanced weapon systems, the modernisation of military infrastructure, and the cultivation of a robust local defence industry. This economic support empowers Israel to create self-sufficiency in defence production, ensuring a constant inflow of cutting-edge weaponry and technological advancements tailored to its specific security requirements.

Additionally, economic assistance enables Israel to focus on technological innovation, giving rise to homegrown advancements in areas such as cyber warfare, missile defence, and unmanned systems. These indigenous developments serve to fortify Israel's military capabilities while stimulating economic growth and fostering technological leadership.

5. Political Influence

Israel's military capabilities are bolstered through the political influence it commands on the world stage, largely due to international support. Diplomatic backing, particularly from influential countries, grants Israel significant political leverage in regional and international forums. This influence allows Israel to articulate its security concerns effectively and shape policy decisions aligning with its defence interests. Furthermore, the support of powerful allies enables Israel to exert pressure on adversaries and neutralise hostile threats diplomatically, indirectly enhancing its military capabilities.

The international recognition and legitimacy garnered through political support also pave the way for international cooperation, joint military exercises, and intelligence sharing. Israel's military partnerships are strengthened by this political influence, fostering collaborative efforts that synergise knowledge, operational tactics, and technological advancements.

Conclusion

International support, spanning diplomatic, technological, intelligence, training, funding, and political dimensions, has been instrumental in shaping Israel's military capabilities. This support, with the United States as a key partner, has provided Israel with advanced weaponry, access to cutting-edge technology, enhanced intelligence capabilities, and operational expertise. It has fortified Israel's qualitative edge, enabling it to project regional power and respond effectively to evolving security challenges.

Moreover, international support has bolstered Israel's defence infrastructure by fostering economic growth, encouraging technological innovation, and underpinning a vibrant defence industry. The influence and legitimacy conferred through diplomatic backing have furthered Israel's political interests and established partnerships crucial to its military superiority.

The impact of international support on Israel's military capabilities reverberates beyond its borders, influencing the complex dynamics of the Israeli-Palestinian conflict and regional security. As Israel navigates the evolving threats in the Middle East, international support continues to play a pivotal role in maintaining its military edge, safeguarding its national security, and reinforcing its position as a key regional player.

CHAPTER 9

The Role of International Community

The conflict between Israel and Palestine has garnered global attention and involvement due to its complex historical background and sensitive political nature. This chapter explores the multifaceted engagement of different countries and organisations, emphasising their diplomatic efforts, economic influence, peacekeeping initiatives, and the significance of international resolutions. Despite ongoing challenges and limitations, the international community is crucial in facilitating a peaceful resolution.

1. Historical Background

The international community's engagement in the Israeli-Palestinian conflict has deep roots, dating back to the establishment of the State of Israel and the consequential displacement of Palestinians. The United Nations' historic partition plan in 1947 and the subsequent recognition of Israel by various countries set the stage for international involvement and exerted global influence over the conflict's trajectory. Since then, numerous states, regional organisations, and international institutions have contributed to resolving the conflict and sought to establish a peaceful coexistence between Israelis and Palestinians.

2. Diplomatic Efforts

Over the years, diplomatic efforts by the international community have played a vital role in seeking a resolution. Institutions such as the United Nations, European Union, and Arab League have worked to bring the parties to the negotiating table and facilitate dialogue. These diplomatic engagements have resulted in significant peace initiatives, ranging from the Oslo Accords to the Camp David Summit, all aiming to establish a two-state solution.

Various frameworks and proposals have been presented, reflecting different approaches and priorities. The Quartet on the Middle East, comprising the United Nations, the United States, the European Union, and Russia, has played a crucial role in mediating peace talks. Parallel to these initiatives, Track II diplomacy, involving academics, civil society organisations, and non-governmental actors, has also contributed to dialogue and confidence-building measures between Israelis and Palestinians.

3. Challenges and Limitations

Despite diplomatic efforts, the international community faces numerous challenges and limitations in resolving the Israeli-Palestinian conflict. Diverse interests among nations, historical biases, and geopolitical considerations often influence individual countries' position in the conflict. These complexities can hinder unity and complicate the resolution process, causing intermittent setbacks.

Negotiations between the parties have faced obstacles due to deep-rooted historical grievances, issues of land, borders, refugees, and the status of Jerusalem. Intransigence, lack of trust, and political changes within the leadership have also presented challenges to achieving progress. Furthermore, the influence of powerful regional or global actors can shape the dynamics of negotiations, exacerbating divisions or impeding meaningful dialogue.

4. Role of Economic Influence

Economic influence is a potent tool in shaping the Israeli-Palestinian conflict. States and organisations employ various economic instruments to exert pressure or incentivise dialogue and peaceful solutions. International trade, investment, and financial aid contribute to the conflict's balance of power and dynamics. If applied judiciously, responsible economic leverage can encourage positive outcomes and promote stability.

International actors have utilised economic incentives and penalties to influence parties involved in the Israeli-Palestinian conflict. Conditionalities in aid and trade agreements have been employed to encourage adherence to peace efforts and humanitarian principles. Conversely, boycott movements or divestment campaigns, such as the Boycott, Divestment, and Sanctions (BDS) movement, have sought to hold Israel accountable for human rights violations and settlement expansion.

Development and infrastructure projects funded by international donors aim to improve the living conditions of Palestinians in the West Bank and Gaza. These initiatives focus on education, healthcare, water management, and job creation, aiming to enhance stability and foster economic opportunities that can contribute to long-term peace.

5. Peacekeeping and Humanitarian Efforts

The international community is crucial in peacekeeping and humanitarian aid to affected populations. United Nations agencies, non-governmental organisations, and humanitarian bodies work tirelessly to mitigate the suffering, provide necessary resources, and develop infrastructure in Gaza and the West Bank. These efforts aim to alleviate the immediate humanitarian impact of the conflict and create conditions conducive to peace.

Thousands of peacekeepers and observers have been deployed to the region under various UN missions, such as the United Nations Truce Supervision Organisation (UNTSO), the United Nations Interim Force in Lebanon (UNIFIL), and the United Nations Disengagement Observer Force (UNDOF). Their presence helps monitor ceasefires, prevent escalations, and facilitate stability.

International organisations provide humanitarian assistance, from emergency relief to long-term development projects. This includes access to clean water, medical services, education, and food security programmes. Grassroots initiatives, supported by international donors, promote coexistence and dialogue at the community level, fostering understanding between Israelis and Palestinians.

6. The Impact of International Resolutions

International resolutions, often passed in the United Nations General Assembly or the Security Council, have historically attempted to shape the trajectory of the conflict. While symbolic in nature, resolutions reflect global consensus on key issues and serve as a foundation for future negotiations. However, the practical implementation of resolutions faces challenges, particularly when Israel's non-compliance with certain resolutions persists, such as the call to halt settlement expansion.

Resolutions like UN Security Council Resolution 242 call for the withdrawal of Israeli armed forces from territories occupied during the Six-Day War, emphasising the importance of a just and lasting peace in the region. Resolutions like UN General Assembly Resolution 194 highlight the right of return for Palestinian refugees and their descendants. These resolutions serve as reference points for peace negotiations and set a precedent for future discussions on borders, refugees, Jerusalem, and security arrangements.

International resolutions also provide a platform for addressing violations of international law, such as settlement construction, the separation barrier, and excessive use of force. The International Court of Justice's advisory opinion on the legality of the wall built by Israel in the West Bank underscores the international community's responsibility to uphold international law and human rights principles.

7. Security Cooperation and Defence Assistance

The international community's role extends to security cooperation and defence assistance. Certain countries provide military aid, training, and support to either Israel or the Palestinians, aiming to ensure stability and security within the region. However, such assistance and cooperation can inadvertently perpetuate the conflict by enhancing the military capacities of the parties involved.

Security cooperation initiatives promote collaboration between Israeli and Palestinian security forces to combat terrorism, improve coordination, and promote stability. International actors invest in capacity-building programmes, professional training, and equipment to enhance the Palestinians' ability to maintain law and order. Balancing assistance to both sides is vital to maintaining credibility and credibility in fostering a fair and sustainable solution.

Conclusion

The role of the international community in the Israeli-Palestinian conflict is complex and multifaceted. While diplomatic efforts, economic influence, peacekeeping initiatives, and humanitarian aid contribute to easing tensions, challenges and limitations persist. Achieving a just and lasting resolution demands sustained engagement, impartiality, and sincere efforts to address the interests and grievances of all parties involved. Only through collective responsibility and a cohesive approach can the international community significantly contribute to a peaceful future in the region.

CHAPTER 10

Assessment of the Involvement and Influence of Various States and Organisations

Regional Actors

The role of regional actors, including Arab countries and neighbouring states, is integral to the Israeli-Palestinian conflict. Historically, Arab countries have offered vocal support to the Palestinian cause, driven by a sense of solidarity with their fellow Arabs. This support varies in its intensity and nature, influenced by Arab states' individual geopolitical concerns, security interests, and domestic political landscapes. Egypt and Jordan stand out due to their unique position as the only Arab states to have signed peace agreements with Israel. These agreements have allowed them to assume diplomatic roles in peace efforts, often mediating or facilitating between Israelis and Palestinians.

Iran, driven by its revolutionary ideology and desire to challenge Israel's regional dominance, has actively supported Palestinian militant groups such as Hamas and Islamic Jihad. This support, including financial aid, weapons, and training, contributes to the complexity of the conflict. Other regional actors, such as Lebanon and Syria, have been involved due to their hosting of significant Palestinian refugee populations and their historical connections to Palestinian resistance movements. However, the political dynamics in these countries, including the influence of Hezbollah in Lebanon and the ongoing civil war in Syria, have posed additional challenges to resolving the Israeli-Palestinian conflict.

International Organisations

International organisations, such as the United Nations (UN) and the European Union (EU), play crucial roles in the Israeli-Palestinian conflict. The UN, through its General Assembly, offers a platform for both Israelis and Palestinians to voice their concerns and perspectives. Over the years, the UN has passed numerous resolutions condemning actions that violate Palestinian rights or hinder the peace process. However, these resolutions often face criticism from Israel and the United States, with both entities accusing the UN of biased treatment.

The United Nations Relief and Works Agency for Palestine Refugees in the Near East (UNRWA) has played a vital humanitarian role, providing education, healthcare, and social services to millions of Palestinian refugees. Its assistance is vital, particularly in areas affected by violence and instability. Meanwhile, the UN Security Council has struggled to reach a consensus on resolutions due to the veto power held by its permanent members, leading to frustration among some member states and delaying meaningful action.

The EU has actively supported peace initiatives and advocated for a two-state solution. It provides significant economic aid to the Palestinian Authority and plays a role in facilitating economic and political development in the region. However, the influence of the EU has been limited by the diverse opinions of its member states and its role as a predominantly non-military actor.

Civil Society and Non-Governmental Organisations (NGOs)

Civil society and non-governmental organisations (NGOs) have played an essential and multifaceted role in the Israeli-Palestinian conflict. These organisations span a wide spectrum, ranging from human rights advocacy groups to peacebuilding organisations. They often engage in grassroots efforts, promoting dialogue, understanding, and reconciliation between Israelis and Palestinians.

Some notable organisations, such as B'Tselem and Breaking the Silence, have faced criticism from pro-Israel groups for providing evidence of human rights violations committed by Israeli authorities. On the other side, organisations like Human Rights Watch and Amnesty International diligently campaign against perceived injustices endured by Palestinians. These organisations shape international public opinion by documenting violations, issuing reports, and advocating for accountability.

In addition to these human rights-focused organisations, other NGOs concentrate on peacebuilding and conflict resolution. Organisations such as Peace Now work towards a just peace and have been instrumental in raising awareness about the settlement issue, advocating for a freeze on settlement expansion, and promoting dialogue between Israelis and Palestinians.

Religious and Cultural Organisations

Religious and cultural organisations, both within the region and globally, actively engage with the Israeli-Palestinian conflict. They often play a role in promoting interfaith dialogue, fostering understanding, and supporting peace initiatives. Jewish organisations, such as J Street and T'ruah, advocate for a peaceful resolution to the conflict, challenging Israeli government policies they perceive as inhibiting progress towards peace.

Muslim organisations, including the Muslim World League and Islamic Relief, work towards addressing the humanitarian needs of Palestinians and promoting justice. They emphasise the significance of Jerusalem as an essential religious site for Muslims and advocate for Palestinian self-determination.

Christian organisations, such as the World Council of Churches, utilise their influence to advocate for Palestinian rights and challenge Israeli policies seen as inhibiting the resolution of the conflict. They promote peace, reconciliation, and respectful coexistence among all religious communities in the region.

Interfaith initiatives, such as the Elijah Interfaith Institute and the King Abdullah bin Abdulaziz International Centre for Interreligious and Intercultural Dialogue, bring together religious leaders and scholars from different faith traditions. These initiatives create spaces for dialogue, fostering understanding and promoting peaceful coexistence among diverse religious communities.

Conclusion

The involvement and influence of various states and organisations in the Israeli-Palestinian conflict are multidimensional and intricate. This analysis has comprehensively assessed their roles, interests, and impact on pursuing a resolution. Understanding the complexities of their involvement is crucial in navigating the path towards a just and lasting peace. By engaging with these diverse stakeholders and acknowledging their perspectives, the international community can create an environment conducive to meaningful dialogue, negotiation, and compromise, ultimately leading to a peaceful resolution.

CHAPTER 11

Examination of the Challenges Faced by Palestinians in Gaining International Support

The struggle for Palestinian self-determination and attaining international support has been complex and arduous. This chapter explores the myriad challenges Palestinians face in garnering widespread global support for their cause. By examining historical factors, political dynamics, and existing power imbalances, we can better understand Palestinians' obstacles to international solidarity.

1. Historical Context

To fully understand the challenges Palestinians face in gaining international support, it is crucial to examine the historical context. The Israeli-Palestinian conflict finds its roots in the British Mandate period, the Balfour Declaration, and the subsequent displacement of Palestinians during the 1948 Nakba. These historical factors have resulted in a deep divide in narratives, making it difficult for some segments of the international community to engage or empathise with the Palestinian struggle fully.

The Nakba, meaning "catastrophe" in Arabic, refers to the dispossession and displacement of Palestinians from their homes and the establishment of the State of Israel. This traumatic event has left a lasting impact on Palestinian identity, memory, and aspirations for self-determination. However, the narrative surrounding the Nakba has often been downplayed or denied by Israel, hindering efforts to gain global support.

2. Influence of Geopolitics

Geopolitics plays a significant role in shaping international responses to the Israeli-Palestinian conflict, posing challenges for Palestinians seeking broad international support. The Middle East is strategically important due to its energy resources and geopolitical significance. As a result, countries often align their stances based on alliances, strategic partnerships, and economic interests, which may result in a limited willingness to support the Palestinian cause or exert pressure on Israel fully.

The United States has been a significant player in the Israeli-Palestinian tragedy, often providing significant financial and military support to Israel. The close relationship between the US and Israel has implications for international support for Palestinians, as the US's role as a veto-wielding member of the UN Security Council can hamper efforts to condemn Israeli actions or call for accountability. Other powerful countries, such as Russia and China, also have their own geopolitical interests in the region, influencing their positions and potential support for Palestinians.

3. Lobbying and Perception Management

Israel has maintained a significant advantage in presenting its narrative and lobbying for its interests on the global stage. Pro-Israel lobbying groups, such as AIPAC in the United States, have exerted considerable influence on policymakers, media outlets, and public opinion. Their well-funded campaigns and public relations efforts have been successful in diminishing Palestinian voices, monopolising the international narrative, and framing the conflict in Israel's favour. This challenge further underscores Palestinians' uphill battle to gain comprehensive international backing.

The influence of pro-Israel lobbying groups also extends to stifling criticism of Israel by labelling it as anti-Semitic or attacking individuals and organisations that support Palestinian rights. This tactic has created a chilling effect on public discourse, making it difficult for individuals and institutions to openly express solidarity with the Palestinian cause without facing potential backlash.

4. Cultural and Religious Divide

The Israeli-Palestinian conflict carries deep religious and cultural undertones, which can influence international support for Palestinians. Jerusalem, with its religious significance to Judaism, Christianity, and Islam, adds another layer of complexity to the issue. These religious connections often shape perceptions and allegiances, creating obstacles for Palestinians seeking to build broad-based alliances. Religious affiliations may sway public opinion and policy decisions in favour of Israel, leading to challenges in garnering universal support for the Palestinian cause.

The geopolitical and historical context should not overshadow the fundamental human rights concerns at the core of the Israeli-Palestinian conflict. While religious and cultural considerations are significant, it is crucial to prioritise the principles of justice, equality, and human rights in seeking international support for the Palestinian cause.

5. *International Relations and Balance of Power*

The balance of power within international relations significantly affects the level of support Palestinians can obtain. Powerful states with vested interests in the region, such as the United States, have historically played a dominant role in shaping international responses to the Israeli-Palestinian conflict. The close alignment between major powers and Israel can limit opportunities for Palestinians to garner widespread support. Veto powers and strategic alliances may undermine efforts to hold Israel accountable for its actions, making it challenging for Palestinians to secure substantial international backing.

Despite these challenges, there have been instances of international solidarity with the Palestinian cause. Grassroots movements, civil society organisations, and individuals have mobilised around the world to advocate for Palestinian rights, putting pressure on governments and international institutions to address the injustices faced by Palestinians. Increased awareness and grassroots activism have the potential to shift the balance of power in favour of Palestinians, prompting governments to reassess their positions and policies.

6. *Influence of Media and Framing*

Media plays a crucial role in shaping public opinion and perceptions of the Israeli-Palestinian conflict. However, media coverage has often been criticised for bias, misrepresentation, and limited inclusion of Palestinian perspectives. The framing of narratives can perpetuate stereotypes, erase Palestinian voices, and prioritise Israeli perspectives, hindering the Palestinian cause from gaining sufficient international traction. Overcoming these challenges necessitates concerted efforts to ensure accurate and balanced media coverage that reflects the conflict's complexity and human rights dimensions.

Social media platforms present new opportunities for Palestinians to share their stories directly, bypassing traditional media gatekeepers. However, social media also poses challenges, as false narratives and targeted online harassment can undermine efforts to raise awareness about the Palestinian struggle.

7. Fragmentation and Lack of Cohesion

Palestinian representation and unity have, at times, been fractured, posing a significant challenge in garnering international support. Internal political divisions, factional struggles, and divergent strategies among Palestinian factions have weakened the overall Palestinian voice. This fragmentation undermines the ability to project a cohesive message and secure sustained international solidarity. Efforts towards reconciliation and unified representation are essential to overcome this challenge and strengthen the Palestinian cause.

Efforts to achieve Palestinian reconciliation and unity must prioritise the engagement and inclusion of all Palestinian factions, as well as the broader range of Palestinian voices, including refugees and marginalised communities. Building a unified front can enhance international support and increase the chances of securing a just resolution to the Israeli-Palestinian conflict.

Conclusion

Gaining widespread international support for the Palestinian cause remains an uphill battle, plagued by complex historical, geopolitical, and perceptual challenges. Understanding and analytically examining these obstacles are crucial for crafting effective strategies to overcome them. Palestinians need cohesive leadership, international solidarity, and continued efforts to raise awareness of the Palestinian struggle's human rights dimensions. It requires concerted actions to counter the influence of lobbying efforts, address cultural and religious divides, navigate geopolitical pressures, ensure fair media representation, and promote internal cohesion. By addressing these challenges head-on, Palestinians may better position themselves to garner the support necessary to achieve their aspirations for self-determination, justice, and a just resolution to the Israeli-Palestinian conflict.

CHAPTER 12

Analysing the Limitations and Impact of International Resolutions

International resolutions have played a significant role in attempting to address the Israeli-Palestinian conflict. These resolutions, adopted by various international bodies, including the United Nations Security Council and the General Assembly, aim to promote peace, justice, and the realisation of the rights of both Israelis and Palestinians. This chapter takes a closer look at the limitations and impact of international resolutions on the Israeli-Palestinian conflict. It explores their legitimacy, practical constraints, and potential to bring about progress.

The Legitimacy of International Resolutions

International resolutions serve as a crucial tool for addressing conflicts between nations, providing a framework for negotiation and diplomacy. In the case of the Israeli-Palestinian conflict, these resolutions carry significant weight as they represent the collective opinion of the international community. They reflect the aspirations of numerous countries and are guided by international law and principles of justice and human rights. While some may question their effectiveness or bias, it is important to recognise their inherent legitimacy as an outcome of democratic decision-making processes. Recognising this legitimacy is crucial as it upholds the principles of multilateralism and encourages compliance with international law.

The Limitations of International Resolutions

1. Non-binding Nature: International resolutions, while having moral authority and setting forth guidelines for conflict resolution, are non-binding in nature. Unlike treaties or legally binding agreements, resolutions lack direct enforcement mechanisms to ensure parties' compliance. As a result, resolutions may be disregarded or implemented selectively, limiting their impact on the ground. This non-binding nature underscores the importance of political will and commitment from the parties to implement the resolutions effectively.

2. Veto Power: The United Nations Security Council, entrusted with maintaining international peace and security, faces limitations due to the veto power held by certain permanent members, namely the United States, Russia, China, France, and the United Kingdom. The use of veto power can hinder the adoption of resolutions favourable to one side or another, leading to a stalemate and preventing the implementation of solutions. This limitation has often been evident in the context of the Israeli-Palestinian conflict, where the United States vetoed certain resolutions critical of Israeli actions. Overcoming these limitations requires a collective commitment to reform the Security Council's veto power, ensuring that resolutions are based on fair and just principles rather than partisan interests.

3. Lack of Consensus: The Israeli-Palestinian conflict encompasses deep-rooted historical, political, and religious dimensions, making consensus among a diverse group of nations challenging. Different interests and priorities can lead to diluted or compromised resolutions that do not fully address the root causes of the conflict. The lack of consensus can sometimes result in resolutions that lack the boldness and specificity required to address the complexities of the Israeli-Palestinian conflict effectively. Resolving these differences and promoting consensus-building efforts are essential to strengthen the impact of international resolutions.

The Impact of International Resolutions

1. Moral Pressure: International resolutions provide a moral framework that pressures the parties involved to abide by the principles of peace, justice, and respect for international law. The global community's consensus on these issues can powerfully shape public opinion and influence political decision-making. The existence of resolutions reaffirms the universal values of human rights, self-determination, and the prohibition of illegal settlement activities. By upholding these human rights principles and international humanitarian law, resolutions hold parties accountable for their actions, enhancing expectations for compliance and moral progress.

2. Legal Basis: International resolutions contribute to the development of international law, providing a legal framework for addressing the Israeli-Palestinian conflict. They establish principles and guidelines that serve as a basis for negotiations, future agreements, and the pursuit of justice and accountability. Resolutions affirm the right to self-determination, the protection of civilians, and the obligations of occupying powers. The legal basis of resolutions promotes stability and predictability, enabling Israelis and Palestinians to seek recourse for

violations and assert their rights in line with established international norms.

3. Confidence-Building Measures: Resolutions can serve as confidence-building measures, fostering an environment conducive to negotiation and peace-building. By delineating principles for a fair and just resolution, resolutions can help establish a foundation for dialogue between the parties involved. Recognizing each party's rights, addressing humanitarian concerns, and endorsing the need for a secure and viable future state for both Israelis and Palestinians can contribute to creating trust and the willingness to engage in constructive dialogue. Additionally, resolutions can pave the way for practical steps, such as exchanging prisoners or implementing ceasefires, to build mutual confidence and ease tensions on the ground.

Conclusion

International resolutions have limitations regarding enforcement power, but their impact on the Israeli-Palestinian conflict should not be underestimated. They provide a moral and legal framework, exerting pressure on the parties involved and shaping public opinion. International resolutions can serve as tools for confidence-building and create a basis for future negotiations. However, to realise their full potential, concerted efforts must be made to address their limitations, such as reforming veto powers and promoting consensus-building among nations. Ultimately, achieving a comprehensive and just resolution to the Israeli-Palestinian conflict requires the commitment and cooperation of all parties involved beyond the constraints of international resolutions alone. By acknowledging these limitations and working collectively to overcome them, the international community can contribute to the pursuit of lasting peace, stability, and justice in the region.

CHAPTER 13

Psychological Warfare and Propaganda

In any conflict, the weapon of information is as powerful as any physical armament. The Israeli-Palestinian conflict is no exception, with psychological warfare and propaganda playing a significant role in shaping public perceptions and influencing international opinion. This chapter aims to delve into the intricacies of psychological war and propaganda employed by both Israelis and Palestinians, examining their methods, impact, and ethical implications.

1. The Information War

The information war in the Israeli-Palestinian conflict is characterised by the extensive use of media channels, social media platforms, and other communication tools to shape narratives and influence public opinion. Both sides employ sophisticated strategies to legitimise their actions, vilify the other party, and garner support from international actors. These tactics include controlling the narrative, manipulating information, and crafting messaging to evoke emotional responses.

The Israeli government, for example, has invested heavily in public relations campaigns to present their actions as self-defence against terrorism. They utilise spokespeople, press releases, and official statements to shape a perception of moral superiority and highlight the threat posed by Palestinian militant groups. On the other hand, Palestinian factions employ various media outlets and online platforms to expose what they view as Israeli aggression and occupation, capitalising on stories of civilian casualties, house demolitions, and restricted access to basic services.

2. Media Coverage and Bias

Media coverage of the Israeli-Palestinian conflict is pivotal in shaping public perception. The role of the media is not only to report events but also to interpret, analyse, and contextualise them. However, biases and sensationalism can often distort the reality on the ground, leading to misrepresentations or oversimplifications. Both Israeli and Palestinian sources strive to influence media narratives, creating an intricate web of selective reporting and manipulation of facts.

For example, some media outlets may focus more on Israeli casualties, painting Palestinians as terrorists, while others may emphasise Palestinian suffering to highlight their victimhood and the injustice of the occupation. These biases influence international public opinion and reinforce pre-existing biases held by audiences. The media also faces challenges in accessing reliable information in conflict zones, leading to errors or reliance on official sources, further exacerbating bias.

3. Psychological Tactics

Psychological tactics are widely deployed to sway public opinion and reinforce the legitimacy of one's own cause. Emotional appeals, narratives of victimhood, and demonisation of the other are common strategies used by both Israelis and Palestinians. Appeals to historical and religious narratives intensify the emotions attached to the conflict, making it even more challenging to find common ground for a peaceful resolution.

For Israelis, the recollection of the Holocaust and a sense of collective trauma are used to justify their quest for security, framing it as a matter of survival for the Jewish people. Palestinians, on the other hand, draw on historical grievances, such as the displacement and dispossession resulting from the creation of the State of Israel, to strengthen their claims for self-determination and justice. These psychological tactics perpetuate a cycle of victimhood and dehumanisation, making it difficult for either side to empathise with the suffering and aspirations of the other.

4. The Impact of Propaganda

Propaganda campaigns in the Israeli-Palestinian conflict have far-reaching consequences. They can shape public opinion, mobilise support or condemnation, and influence political decision-making. The use of propaganda can solidify existing biases, hinder objective analysis, and impede efforts towards peacebuilding and reconciliation.

Internationally, heavily skewed and selective narratives can sway public opinion, polarising support for one side over the other. This polarisation may translate into diplomatic and political actions that hinder the prospects of a negotiated settlement. Domestically, propaganda campaigns contribute to the entrenchment of positions, making it difficult for alternative perspectives and voices of moderation to gain traction. The impact of propaganda is not limited to the conflict's immediate participants but extends to the broader international community, shaping their perceptions and responses to the conflict.

5. Ethical Implications

The employment of psychological warfare and propaganda in the Israeli-Palestinian conflict raises important ethical concerns. Deliberate misinformation, manipulation of images, and sensationalism can exacerbate tensions, the dehumanisation of the other, and the perpetuation of conflict. Engaging in ethical journalism and critical media literacy is crucial to counteract the impact of propaganda and create a space for informed and nuanced understanding.

Journalists and media professionals have a responsibility to present accurate and balanced information, ensuring that their reporting is thorough, fact-checked, and mindful of the consequences it may have. Additionally, media consumers must be proactive in critically evaluating the information they encounter and seeking out diverse perspectives. Promoting media literacy education is essential in equipping individuals with the tools to discern fact from fiction, challenge biases, and foster empathy and understanding among various communities.

Furthermore, it is essential to analyse the specific forms of psychological warfare and propaganda utilised by different parties in the conflict. Israelis heavily rely on the concept of "Hasbara," a term referring to public relations efforts aimed at presenting Israel and its policies in a positive light. Through Hasbara, Israeli authorities seek to counter negative narratives, combat delegitimization, and portray themselves as a democracy acting in self-defence against terrorism. This approach involves engaging with international media, organising press tours and interviews, and utilising social media influencers to disseminate their messaging.

Palestinian factions, on the other hand, employ various strategies to raise awareness about their aspirations for statehood and to highlight the occupation's adverse effects. They rely on visual storytelling, sharing images and videos through social media platforms to evoke sympathy and mobilise support worldwide. These images often depict scenes of violence, displacement, and the everyday struggles faced by Palestinians living under occupation. Additionally, Palestinian propaganda often utilises historical narratives, invoking the Nakba (catastrophe) and other significant events to reinforce their claims of injustice.

It is crucial to recognise that psychological warfare and propaganda are not exclusive to the Israeli and Palestinian governments. Non-governmental organisations (NGOs), advocacy groups, and individuals also play critical roles in shaping narratives and influencing public opinion. NGOs like Human Rights Watch, Amnesty International, and B'Tselem are engaged in gathering and disseminating information about human rights violations, seeking to hold both Israelis and Palestinians accountable.

Throughout the conflict's history, the utilisation of social media has become increasingly prominent. Individuals and grassroots movements often utilise online platforms to share stories, documentaries, and personal testimonies. This decentralised approach allows for unique perspectives to reach a global audience, but it also exposes information consumers to a vast array of partially or entirely false content. The circulation of misinformation, doctored images, and misleading narratives on social media platforms has further complicated the information landscape and intensified the propaganda war.

Conclusion

Psychological warfare and propaganda are formidable tools employed by both Israelis and Palestinians to influence public opinion, shape narratives, and garner support. The extent and effectiveness of these tactics can have profound implications on efforts towards peace and reconciliation. Recognising the strategic utilisation of information in the Israeli-Palestinian conflict is essential for developing media literacy, critical analysis, and balanced perspectives. By fostering a more nuanced understanding of the complexities at hand, we can strive to create an environment conducive to dialogue, empathy, and, ultimately, a just and lasting resolution.

CHAPTER 14

Exploration of the Information War in the Israeli-Palestinian Conflict

The Israeli-Palestinian conflict occurs on the physical battleground and in the domain of information and perception. This chapter explores the intricate landscape of the information war surrounding this long-lasting conflict. It aims to provide a thorough understanding of both sides' methods, strategies, and impact of the media and propaganda campaigns.

1. Historical Context

The significance of the information war in the Israeli-Palestinian conflict can be understood by examining its historical development. From the early stages of the conflict, both Israel and the Palestinians recognised the influence of public opinion and sought to shape narratives that aligned with their goals.

Throughout the years, various media outlets have played a role in shaping public perception. During the early years of the conflict, biased reporting by international media outlets fuelled narratives favouring either the Israeli or Palestinian perspective, perpetuating stereotypes and amplifying divisions. However, with the advent of more independent and critical journalism, alternative narratives and diverse perspectives have emerged, challenging the dominant narratives of both sides.

2. Media Coverage

Media coverage plays a significant role in influencing global opinion on the Israeli-Palestinian conflict. However, the media faces challenges in providing unbiased reporting due to political pressure, access limitations, and safety concerns. Journalists operating in the region often confront difficulties in gaining access to information and affected areas, facing potential risks to their safety.

Additionally, media bias can also shape coverage. In the case of the Israeli-Palestinian conflict, ideological leanings, historical perspectives, and political pressures can influence media outlets' reporting. It is essential for journalists to maintain ethical standards, ensure a diversity of perspectives, and fact-cheque information to provide accurate and balanced coverage.

3. Propaganda Techniques

Both sides of the conflict employ various propaganda techniques to influence public opinion. Selective reporting, where specific incidents are highlighted or omitted, aims to shape narratives that serve the respective agendas. Emotional appeals, through the use of images and personal stories, seek to evoke sympathy or anger and garner support for one side. Demonisation of the opponent is another widely used tactic, portraying the adversary as evil or barbaric to dehumanise them and legitimise one's own actions.

Historical narratives are manipulated to reinforce the perceived legitimacy of each side's claims. For example, Israel highlights its historical and biblical connections to the land, while Palestinians emphasise their roots and right to self-determination. These narratives are often oversimplified and exclude the complex historical and political factors contributing to the conflict, perpetuating divisions and entrenching long-standing beliefs.

Additionally, both Israel and the Palestinians deploy strategies to control information within their respective territories. Governments may implement media censorship, control internet access, or restrict journalists' movements, limiting the information available to the public. This censorship further contributes to the information war by inhibiting the free flow of information and restricting critical analysis.

4. *Social Media and Online Warfare*

With the rise of social media platforms, the information war in the Israeli-Palestinian conflict has intensified. Social media has become vital for disseminating information, shaping public opinion, and mobilising support. Previously inaccessible, individuals now have the ability to share their perspectives, raise awareness, and amplify narratives that align with their positions.

However, social media platforms face challenges in moderating content and preventing the spread of misinformation. The boundary between freedom of expression and hate speech can be blurred, making it difficult to regulate the content shared online. Fake accounts, bots, and paid trolls further complicate the information space, manipulating narratives and amplifying propaganda. These tactics aim to influence public opinion through the sheer volume and repetition of content rather than its accuracy. The influence of social media in the information war underscores the need for critical media literacy and efforts to ensure information accuracy.

5. Impacts on Public Perception

The information war significantly influences public perception of the Israeli-Palestinian conflict, both domestically and globally. Media narratives and propaganda campaigns shape attitudes towards the conflict, its actors, and potential solutions. These perceptions, in turn, impact political decisions, international support, and peace efforts.

Public opinion can be polarised, with individuals aligning themselves with one side based on the dominant narratives they encounter. This polarisation hinders constructive dialogue and understanding, making it challenging to bridge the divide between the Israelis and Palestinians. Additionally, the global dimension of the conflict and its connection to broader geopolitical dynamics further complicates public perception and attempts at resolution.

Moreover, the impact of the information war extends beyond public opinion to policy-making processes. Decision-makers are not immune to the influence of media narratives and propaganda techniques. These factors can shape their understanding of the conflict, bias their perspectives, and influence their policy choices. The information war's effect on policy-making processes adds another layer of complexity to resolving the Israeli-Palestinian conflict.

6. Fact-checking and Independent Verification

Amid conflicting narratives, fact-checking and independent verification play a crucial role in the information war. Independent media outlets, non-governmental organisations (NGOs), and fact-checking organisations provide critical analysis and reliable information to counter misinformation and propaganda. They scrutinise claims, verify sources, and offer alternative perspectives to ensure a more accurate understanding of the conflict.

However, the challenges faced by these organisations should not be overlooked. Limited resources, access restrictions, and political pressures can hinder conducting thorough fact-checking. Additionally, the highly polarised nature of the Israeli-Palestinian conflict often leads to defensive reactions when confronted with contrary information. People tend to seek out information that confirms their beliefs and reject information that challenges their worldview, making it difficult to break the cycle of misinformation.

Efforts are being made to establish a network of organisations collaborating to fact-check and verify information related to the Israeli-Palestinian conflict. These initiatives help dispel false narratives and foster transparency, accountability, and critical thinking. By promoting independent verification, these efforts aim to counter the information war's impact on public perception and facilitate a more informed and nuanced understanding of the conflict.

7. *Countering Misinformation*

Countering misinformation is essential to facilitating a more nuanced understanding of the conflict. Governments, organisations, and individuals engage in various initiatives to promote accurate information and combat propaganda. Educational programmes, media literacy campaigns, and grassroots movements aim to bridge the divide, encourage critical thinking, and facilitate dialogue based on verified facts.

However, countering misinformation is not without its challenges. The highly polarised nature of the conflict often leads to defensive reactions when confronted with contrary information. Echo chambers, where people surround themselves with like-minded individuals and outlets reinforcing their beliefs, can perpetuate misinformation and hinder open dialogue.

To address these challenges, efforts must be made to create spaces for open and respectful dialogue, encourage critical media literacy, and promote fact-based discussions. Collaborative initiatives involving stakeholders from both sides of the conflict could play an essential role in countering misinformation and fostering understanding.

Conclusion

The information war in the Israeli-Palestinian conflict perpetuates a cycle of narratives, competing truths, and biased perceptions. Understanding how information is manipulated and disseminated is vital to developing a comprehensive view of the conflict. By critically analysing the information war, individuals can cultivate a more nuanced understanding and guard against manipulation, fostering an environment conducive to constructive dialogue and conflict resolution. Efforts to promote fact-checking, independent verification, and countering misinformation are crucial in ensuring a more accurate understanding of the Israeli-Palestinian conflict. Collaborative initiatives involving media organisations, fact-checking organisations, NGOs, and individuals from both sides of the conflict can contribute to countering misinformation and propaganda.

Education plays a key role in countering misinformation. Teaching critical media literacy skills from a young age empowers individuals to evaluate information critically, recognise bias, and seek out diverse perspectives. Educational programmes can provide students with the tools to navigate the complex information landscape and develop a more nuanced understanding of the conflict.

Media literacy campaigns also potentially foster a more informed public discourse. These campaigns can educate the public about common propaganda techniques, encourage fact-checking, and promote responsible information sharing. By empowering individuals to be critical information consumers, media literacy campaigns counter misinformation and shape a more accurate understanding of the Israeli-Palestinian conflict.

Collaboration among different stakeholders is crucial in countering the information war. Governments, media organisations, fact-checking organisations, NGOs, and individuals must cooperate to promote accurate information and counter-propaganda. Sharing resources, expertise, and information can strengthen fact-checking efforts and ensure a more comprehensive conflict analysis.

Engaging in dialogue and promoting understanding across communities is another critical aspect of countering the information war. Creating spaces for open and respectful conversations between Israelis and Palestinians can help break down stereotypes, challenge entrenched beliefs, and foster empathy. Grassroots initiatives, community discussions, and peace-building programmes can facilitate dialogue and bridge the divide between the two sides.

Ultimately, countering misinformation and propaganda in the Israeli-Palestinian conflict requires a multifaceted approach. Fact-checking, media literacy, collaboration, and dialogue all play essential roles in shaping a more accurate and nuanced understanding of the conflict. By challenging false narratives, promoting critical thinking, and facilitating open dialogue, efforts to counter the information war can contribute to more informed public opinion and create a foundation for peace and resolution in the Israeli-Palestinian conflict.

CHAPTER 15

Analysis of Media Coverage and its Impact on Public Perceptions

In today's globalised and interconnected world, media plays a pivotal role in shaping public perceptions of conflicts and influencing popular opinion. The Israeli-Palestinian conflict is no exception. This chapter will analyse the media coverage surrounding the conflict, exploring its nuances, biases, and impact on public perceptions.

1. The Power of Media in Shaping Public Opinion

Media outlets, whether traditional print, television, or online platforms, have the ability to disseminate information, images, and narratives that significantly shape public perceptions. Their selection of storeys, framing techniques, and editorial decisions can influence how audiences interpret and understand the complex and multifaceted Israeli-Palestinian struggle.

2. Bias and Objectivity in Media

Media bias is an inherent challenge in reporting on conflicts, including the Israeli-Palestinian situation. Bias can manifest through selecting specific events to report, the framing of stories, the language used, and the choice of interviewees. Both Israeli and Palestinian media outlets, as well as international media, may exhibit bias, unintentionally or intentionally influencing public perception by presenting a particular narrative or viewpoint.

a) Israeli Bias: Israeli media outlets, while diverse, may tend to focus more on Israeli perspectives, emphasising security concerns, acts of terrorism, and the impact of Palestinian resistance groups. This emphasis can reinforce an "us versus them" narrative, further deepening divisions and consolidating existing biases. It is important to note that this bias can be attributed to Israeli society's pervasive security concerns and the impact of ongoing violence.

b) Palestinian Bias: Similarly, Palestinian media outlets may prioritise narratives that highlight Israeli aggression, human rights violations, and the plight of Palestinians under occupation. This emphasis can perpetuate feelings of victimhood and resentment, contributing to a narrative that devalues Israeli security concerns. This bias is influenced by the historical dispossession and the ongoing occupation experienced by the Palestinians, which has shaped their collective narrative.

c) International Bias: International media outlets, especially those with political or ideological leanings, may approach the conflict with their own biases. These biases can influence the selection of storeys to cover or omit, shaping public opinions in their respective countries or regions. Political alliances, historical connections, and geopolitical interests often influence international media coverage of the Israeli-Palestinian conflict.

3. The Role of International Media

International media outlets often sway considerably in shaping public perceptions due to their wider reach and influence. Their portrayal of events and individuals can significantly impact public opinion in various countries. However, it is crucial to scrutinise international media coverage to assess any potential biases or gaps in understanding.

a) Simplification and Stereotyping: International media may sometimes rely on simplified narratives and stereotypes, portraying the conflict as a religious or ethnic clash. This simplification can lead to a distorted understanding of the complexities involved and perpetuate divisive narratives. The Israeli-Palestinian conflict is a deeply rooted political and territorial dispute, encompassing historical, cultural, and religious dimensions that need to be acknowledged.

b) Framing Techniques: International media outlets may use framing techniques, such as selective reporting, emphasising specific incidents or perspectives, or framing events as part of a larger global struggle. These framing techniques can subtly shape public perceptions and influence attitudes towards the Israeli-Palestinian conflict. The framing of the conflict as a binary struggle or as one component of a broader geopolitical landscape affects how audiences interpret and engage with the issue.

4. Social Media and Alternative News Sources

With the rise of social media platforms, individuals have gained the ability to contribute to the narrative surrounding the Israeli-Palestinian conflict. Social media can provide alternative perspectives and voices that challenge mainstream media coverage. However, it is essential to critically evaluate the veracity and reliability of information shared through these channels.

a) Echo Chambers and Confirmation Bias: Social media platforms can facilitate the formation of echo chambers—spaces where individuals are exposed only to content that aligns with their pre-existing beliefs. This confirmation bias can reinforce one-sided perspectives and hinder a comprehensive understanding of the conflict. Algorithms and personal preferences algorithmically shape users' feeds, polarising opinions and limited exposure to diverse viewpoints.

b) Misinformation and "Fake News": Social media platforms are susceptible to the spread of misinformation and "fake news" surrounding the Israeli-Palestinian conflict. Rapidly disseminating inaccurate or biased information can exacerbate divisions, ignite conflicts, and further polarise public opinion. The lack of gatekeeping mechanisms and the viral nature of platform content often make it difficult for users to discern reliable information from misinformation.

5. Impact on Public Perceptions

Media coverage holds immense power in shaping public perceptions, and biased or one-sided reporting can reinforce pre-existing beliefs, stereotypes, and prejudices. This consolidation of existing biases can hinder productive dialogue and understanding between Israeli and Palestinian communities, as well as among international observers.

a) Emotional Appeal and Identification: Media coverage that emphasises human suffering, personal stories, and emotional narratives can elicit strong emotional responses from audiences. These emotions can influence public perceptions and attitudes, encouraging empathy and understanding or deepening animosity and bias. Personal narratives that humanise the experiences of individuals from both sides of the conflict can foster empathy and challenge simplistic stereotypes.

b) Polarisation and Divisions: Biased media coverage, particularly with social media echo chambers, can deepen divisions and polarise public opinion. As people gravitate towards sources that reinforce their viewpoints, fostering constructive dialogue and finding common ground for resolving the conflict becomes challenging. Efforts to encourage media literacy, critical thinking, and exposure to diverse perspectives can help counteract polarisation.

6. The Responsibility of Media Outlets

Media outlets are crucial in providing fair and accurate coverage of the Israeli-Palestinian conflict. They should strive to present multiple perspectives, avoid sensationalism, verify information, and promote ethical journalism. By doing so, media outlets can contribute to a more informed public discourse, foster empathy, and encourage a deeper understanding of the conflict and its complexities. Efforts to include a range of voices, provide historical context, and engage with local communities can help counteract biases and provide a more comprehensive perspective.

Conclusion

Media coverage of the Israeli-Palestinian conflict significantly shapes public perceptions. Biases in reporting, framing techniques, and the influence of social media platforms can all consolidate existing biases and divisions. It is vital for media outlets to maintain objectivity, present multiple perspectives, and ensure accurate reporting to foster informed discussions and a deeper understanding among the public. Audiences, on their part, should engage critically with media coverage, rely on diverse sources, and actively seek out accurate and balanced information to form a comprehensive and nuanced view of the conflict.

CHAPTER 16

Discussion on The Use of Psychological Tactics By Both Sides

In the ongoing Israeli-Palestinian conflict, the use of psychological tactics by both sides cannot be underestimated. These tactics are strategic tools employed to shape public opinion, influence narratives, and strengthen the respective parties' positions. This chapter delves deeper into the various techniques utilised by Israeli and Palestinian actors in the psychological realm and examines their implications.

Historical Context

To understand the psychological tactics employed in the conflict, examining the historical context in which they have evolved is essential. Both Israelis and Palestinians have a long history of utilising methods to shape public opinion within their constituencies and international communities. These methods have been refined, adapting to evolving technologies and changing political environments.

Over the years, both sides have relied on various psychological techniques to establish and maintain their narratives. The Zionist movement, which ultimately led to the creation of the State of Israel, utilised strategies such as emphasising the historical and religious connection of Jews to the land of Palestine, creating a sense of national identity and unity. On the other hand, through their national and liberation movements, Palestinians employed tactics like emphasising historical narratives of displacement and collective trauma, invoking the struggle for self-determination.

Media Manipulation

One of the most significant aspects of psychological tactics in the Israeli-Palestinian conflict involves media manipulation. Both Israeli and Palestinian actors skillfully leverage various mediums, including television, radio, newspapers, and, more recently, social media networks, to disseminate their narratives and shape public perceptions. This often involves strategically highlighting specific events, carefully selecting images that evoke emotional responses, and employing narratives that elicit sympathy, anger, or outrage.

For example, media outlets on both sides have been known to focus on stories that reinforce their respective viewpoints while downplaying or ignoring events that challenge their narratives. Palestinians often highlight incidents of Israeli aggression, illegal settlements, or forced displacement, aiming to evoke international solidarity and condemnation. Israelis, on the other hand, emphasise acts of terrorism, rocket attacks, or threats to internal security, seeking empathy and support for their defensive actions.

Demonisation and Dehumanisation

Demonisation and dehumanisation of the other is a prevalent tactic employed by both sides. Israelis often portray Palestinian resistance as terrorism, while Palestinians frequently depict Israelis as oppressors, colonisers, or occupiers. These tactics create an Otherness, portraying the opponent as inherently evil, barbaric, or threatening. By dehumanising the other, these tactics seek to foster fear and hatred and reinforce narratives that justify or escalate acts of violence.

The demonisation process often involves simplifying complex historical and political realities into stark contrasts between good and evil, reinforcing existing prejudices and stereotypes. Israelis often associate Palestinians with violence, terrorism, and religious extremism, while Palestinians highlight Israel's military superiority and policies of occupation, segregation, and discrimination. These portrayals create rigid divisions, making establishing empathy or seeking common ground harder.

Victimhood and Martyrdom

Another crucial psychological tactic is the projection of victimhood and martyrdom. Both Israelis and Palestinians utilise narratives that depict their respective people as victims of aggression, injustice, and oppression. These narratives consolidate collective identity, foster a sense of resilience, and rally support from their constituencies. Each side seeks to gain international sympathy and support by framing themselves as the victims.

For Palestinians, the narrative of victimhood revolves around the historical displacement of Palestinians during the creation of Israel in

1948, the ongoing occupation, and the alleged violations of human rights. The memory of the Nakba (the Palestinian catastrophe) is a foundational element of the Palestinian national identity. Israelis, on the other hand, highlight the Holocaust and historical persecution of Jews, grounding their victimhood narrative in the need for a secure homeland.

This emphasis on victimhood has its roots in the collective memory and trauma experienced by both sides. It perpetuates a sense of victimhood, reinforcing the belief that their suffering is unique and justifying the use of violence or self-defence.

Weaponising Fear and Trauma

Both sides have been known to exploit fear and trauma to advance their agendas. Israelis often highlight security threats they face, emphasising instances of violence against their citizens or the continuous rocket attacks. The rhetoric of existential threats reinforces the narrative of a vulnerable Jewish state surrounded by hostile neighbours. Palestinians, on the other hand, reference historical trauma, ongoing occupation, and the impact of collective punishment. This includes experiences of checkpoints, house demolitions, land confiscation, and restrictions on movement. These narratives aim to evoke international empathy and support for their struggle for self-determination.

The weaponisation of fear and trauma is not limited to local communities but also extends to international actors. By emphasising security concerns, Israelis seek understanding and support for their controversial policies, such as border controls and military offensives. Palestinians leverage their collective trauma to paint themselves as the victims of historical injustice, hoping to garner international sympathy and condemnation of Israeli actions.

International Influence

Psychological tactics extend beyond the local context, with both Israelis and Palestinians attempting to shape international perceptions. They engage in strategic diplomacy, lobbying efforts, and public relations campaigns to garner support from foreign governments, NGOs, and the global community. These tactics leverage narratives, images, and metrics that resonate with international audiences to influence policy decisions, secure economic aid, and maintain diplomatic legitimacy.

For instance, Israel portrays itself as a democratic and technologically advanced nation while highlighting its contributions to global security, intelligence sharing, and innovation. In contrast, Palestinians seek to portray themselves as victims of Israeli aggression, focusing on human rights violations, restrictions on movement, and the need for international intervention to achieve justice and self-determination.

Impacts and Ethical Considerations

The use of psychological tactics in the Israeli-Palestinian conflict has profound impacts on individuals directly involved, as well as the broader societies affected. These tactics can manipulate emotions, perpetuate deep-rooted biases, and hinder the possibility of empathetic understanding or reconciliation. The ethical considerations surrounding psychological tactics necessitate critical analysis, considering the potential consequences on individuals' mental well-being, social cohesion, and the pursuit of a just and lasting peace.

To address the ethical considerations, it is vital for all parties, including governments, media organisations, and civil society groups, to promote responsible reporting, empathy-driven narratives, and inclusive dialogue. Recognising the humanity and complexity of individuals on both sides of the conflict can help break down barriers and create spaces for understanding, negotiation, and reconciliation.

Conclusion

The employment of psychological tactics by both Israelis and Palestinians in the Israeli-Palestinian conflict highlights the complexity and intensity of their struggle. Understanding and analysing these tactics in depth is crucial for comprehending the dynamics shaping public opinion and the challenges they pose to achieving a peaceful resolution. Acknowledging the intertwined use of media manipulation, demonisation, victimhood, fear, trauma, and international influence helps lay the foundation for a more profound engagement with these psychological forces. Only through such engagement can progress be made towards a more constructive dialogue, empathy-driven perspectives, and the eventual emergence of a just and lasting peace.

CHAPTER 17

The Role of Arab Governments

Arab governments have played a significant and complex role in the Israeli-Palestinian conflict since its inception. Their involvement and stance on the issue have shaped the dynamics of the conflict and influenced the aspirations of the Palestinian people. In this chapter, we will examine the various dimensions of the role of Arab governments, their interests in the conflict, the challenges they face in supporting the Palestinians, and the impact of their actions on the overall landscape.

Arab Interests and Stance

The Israeli-Palestinian conflict holds a special place in the hearts and minds of Arab governments due to a variety of factors. Firstly, the issue resonates deeply with the Arab and Muslim identities, as Jerusalem holds religious and cultural significance for the entire Islamic world. The aspiration for a Palestinian state with East Jerusalem as its capital is seen as a fundamental demand for justice and rights.

Secondly, the Arab world views the Palestinian struggle as a symbol of liberation and justice, representing the broader struggle against foreign occupation. Arab governments consistently emphasise the importance of self-determination for the Palestinian people and advocate for an independent and sovereign Palestinian state in the occupied territories.

Furthermore, the Israeli-Palestinian conflict plays a critical role in the Arab world's political discourse and serves as a unifying issue. Arab governments often leverage the Palestinian cause to strengthen their legitimacy and garner public support. The conflict is seen as a means to rally Arab populations behind their governments and deflect attention from internal challenges. By aligning themselves with the Palestinian cause, Arab governments can assert their commitment to Arab nationalism and demonstrate solidarity with the broader Arab public.

Lastly, the Israeli-Palestinian conflict has significant geopolitical implications for the region. Arab governments recognise that a just and lasting resolution to the conflict is essential for regional stability and security. The unresolved nature of the conflict continues to impact the dynamics of the Middle East, influencing inter-Arab relations, Arab-Israeli relations, and even the broader Arab world's relationship with the international community.

Arab governments have maintained a primarily supportive stance towards the Palestinians, both at the diplomatic and grassroots levels. They have consistently called for an end to the Israeli occupation, the establishment of a viable Palestinian state, and the right of Palestinian refugees to return to their homes. This support has been expressed through diplomatic efforts, financial aid and resources, and various political and diplomatic forums such as the Arab League and the Organisation of Islamic Cooperation.

Challenges Faced by Arab Governments

Despite their supportive stance, Arab governments have faced numerous challenges in effectively supporting the Palestinians. One of the primary challenges lies in the internal divisions among Arab states. Historical rivalries, ideological differences, and conflicting national interests have often hampered a unified and cohesive approach towards the conflict. This lack of unity has weakened the collective Arab bargaining power and limited their ability to influence events.

The divisions within the Arab world have been further exacerbated by the emergence of different political systems and leadership styles among Arab governments. Some governments, particularly those with autocratic regimes, have used the Israeli-Palestinian conflict as a strategic tool to divert attention from domestic issues, suppress political dissent, or justify repressive measures. These actions have created further obstacles to achieving a unified Arab stance and undermined the ability of Arab governments to support the Palestinian cause effectively.

Moreover, Arab governments have had to contend with competing regional priorities. In recent years, the emergence of new regional power dynamics and threats, such as the rise of extremist groups and inter-Arab conflicts, have diverted attention and resources away from the Israeli-Palestinian conflict. The need to address these pressing issues has sometimes overshadowed the Palestinian cause, forcing Arab governments to prioritise other matters.

Furthermore, external pressures from powerful actors can significantly impact Arab governments' policies and actions regarding the Israeli-Palestinian conflict. These pressures can come from countries supporting Israel, international organisations, or even regional powers with different agendas. Some Arab governments have faced economic and political pressure to limit their support for the Palestinians or to normalise relations with Israel, creating intricate diplomatic challenges and trade-offs.

The Role of Arab Governments in Peace Initiatives

Arab governments have played a vital role in advocating for peace between Israelis and Palestinians and have been actively involved in peace initiatives and negotiations. The 2002 Arab Peace Initiative, initially proposed by Saudi Arabia and endorsed by the Arab League, demonstrated a collective Arab commitment to finding a peaceful solution to the conflict. The initiative presented a comprehensive peace plan that offered normalised relations with Israel in exchange for Israeli withdrawal from all occupied territories and the establishment of an independent Palestinian state with East Jerusalem as its capital. Although this initiative did not achieve its intended outcome, it served as a meaningful demonstration of the Arab governments' commitment to a peaceful resolution.

Arab governments have also been involved in mediation efforts, acting as intermediaries between Israeli and Palestinian leaders. This role can be challenging given the asymmetry in power dynamics and the history of mistrust between the parties. Nonetheless, Arab governments have sought to leverage their influence to bridge the gaps and facilitate dialogue.

In addition to promoting peace through diplomatic channels, Arab governments have supported Palestinian efforts to gain international recognition and bring the conflict to the international community's attention. They have played active roles in international organisations, such as the United Nations, advocating for Palestinian rights and pushing for resolutions that condemn Israeli policies and actions. Arab governments have also supported the Palestinians' pursuit of justice through legal avenues, including bringing cases against Israel to international courts.

Conclusion

Arab governments hold a crucial and complex position in the Israeli-Palestinian conflict, reflecting the shared aspirations and interests of the Arab world in supporting the Palestinian cause. However, they face various challenges, including internal divisions, competing interests, and external pressures, which impact their ability to support the Palestinians effectively. Nonetheless, Arab governments continue to play an essential role in advocating for a just and lasting peace, supporting diplomatic efforts, mobilising international support for the Palestinian people, and reinforcing the significance of the Palestinian cause within the broader regional context. Despite the hurdles they face, Arab governments remain committed to the vision of an independent Palestinian state, with East Jerusalem as its capital, and continue to work towards realising this goal.

CHAPTER 18

Evaluation of the Impact of Arab Support or Lack Thereof on Palestinian Aspirations

In the complex and protracted Israeli-Palestinian conflict, the role of Arab governments has been a crucial factor in shaping the trajectory of Palestinian aspirations. This chapter aims to analyse and evaluate the impact of Arab support or the lack thereof on the realisation of Palestinian goals for self-determination and statehood. It provides a detailed examination of the historical, geopolitical, economic, and strategic considerations that influence Arab governments' positions towards the Palestinian cause.

1. *Historical Context*

To understand the present dynamics, it is necessary to delve into the history of Arab support for the Palestinian cause. Following the 1948 Arab-Israeli War and the establishment of the state of Israel, Arab countries expressed solidarity with the Palestinians and their aspirations for independence. Arab support was driven by a strong sense of pan-Arab nationalism and a desire to prevent further Israeli territorial expansion.

The 1967 Six-Day War further heightened Arab states' commitment to the Palestinian cause as they saw Israel occupying territories recognised as part of the future Palestinian state. However, subsequent conflicts and shifting regional dynamics have influenced the level and consistency of Arab support.

2. Geopolitical Considerations:

The geopolitical landscape of the Middle East significantly shapes Arab governments' decisions regarding support for the Palestinians. Internal and external challenges, competing interests, and regional rivalries often influence Arab policies towards Palestine. Some Arab countries prioritise their national security concerns and believe that supporting the Palestinians might jeopardise their relationships with significant powers or regional actors. For instance, countries like Egypt and Jordan have prioritised their respective peace treaties with Israel, impacting their level of support for the Palestinian cause. Similarly, countries like Saudi Arabia and the United Arab Emirates, which share concerns about Iran's regional influence, have shown signs of shifting priorities, leading to a recalibration of their support for the Palestinians.

3. Arab Peace Initiative:

The Arab Peace Initiative, first introduced by Saudi Arabia in 2002, represents a notable development in Arab Palestinian support. This initiative offered comprehensive peace, recognition, and normalisation of relations between Arab states and Israel in exchange for an end to the Israeli occupation and the establishment of an independent Palestinian state. Adopted by the Arab League, the initiative aimed to provide a united front in supporting Palestinian aspirations. However, with ongoing conflicts, differing interpretations, and a lack of progress in peace negotiations, critics argue that the initiative's impact on the ground has been limited. The lack of a meaningful breakthrough in the Israeli-Palestinian peace process has tested the commitment of some Arab countries to the Arab Peace Initiative, leading some observers to question its efficacy.

4. Economic and Financial Assistance:

Arab support for the Palestinians also manifests through financial aid and economic assistance to the Palestinian Authority. Arab countries, particularly those in the Gulf region, have provided substantial financial support to the Palestinians, aiding their infrastructure development and economic stability. This assistance is crucial for the Palestinian Authority to provide essential services and maintain a functioning administration. However, the sustainability and effectiveness of such assistance have faced challenges due to changing regional dynamics, economic constraints, and political disagreements among Arab countries. Financial aid to the Palestinians is often contingent upon political considerations and influenced by various factors, including domestic priorities, political stability, and regional alliances.

5. Political and Diplomatic Support

Political and diplomatic backing from Arab governments through international forums and resolutions is another significant aspect of Arab support for the Palestinian cause. Arab states have often used their influence at the United Nations, the Arab League, and other international platforms to advance Palestinian interests and condemn Israel's policies. This support helps maintain the visibility of the Palestinian cause on the international stage and raises awareness about their struggle for self-determination. Arab countries have been instrumental in pushing for resolutions that condemn Israeli settlements, uphold Palestinian rights, and call for the implementation of a two-state solution. However, the effectiveness and impact of these resolutions are limited by political divisions, regional dynamics, and the ability of the international community to implement them.

6. Challenges and Limitations:

Despite the historical significance of Arab support for the Palestinian cause, there have been challenges and limitations. Internal divisions among Arab states, competing national interests, and the prioritisation of regional stability have, at times, hampered the level and effectiveness of Arab support. The Arab world, itself grappling with political instability, economic challenges, and domestic demands, faces constraints that can limit its ability to exert influence on the Israeli-Palestinian conflict. Furthermore, changing geopolitical dynamics, such as the normalisation of relations between some Arab countries and Israel, have raised questions about the consistency of Arab support for Palestinian aspirations. The Abraham Accords signed between Israel, the United Arab Emirates, Bahrain, Sudan, and Morocco have signalled a shift in the traditional Arab position, with these countries choosing to normalise relations with Israel without significant progress on the Israeli-Palestinian peace process.

Conclusion:

A comprehensive evaluation of the impact of Arab support or lack thereof on Palestinian aspirations reveals a complex interplay of historical, geopolitical, economic, and strategic factors. Arab support for the Palestinian cause has been influenced by regional dynamics, domestic challenges, and competing interests, resulting in varying levels of commitment. Despite financial aid, political solidarity, and diplomatic efforts, these factors have often limited the effectiveness and consistency of Arab support for Palestinian aspirations. Moving forward, it is crucial for Arab governments to remain committed and unified in their support, ensuring a just and lasting resolution to the Israeli-Palestinian conflict and the fulfilment of Palestinian aspirations for self-determination and statehood. The evolving regional dynamics and shifting priorities of Arab governments necessitate reevaluating strategies and approaches to ensure that the Palestinian cause remains at the forefront of regional and international agendas.

CHAPTER 19

Discussion on the Challenges Faced by Arab Governments in Supporting the Palestinians

The Israeli-Palestinian conflict is not confined to the borders of Palestine and Israel; it is a regional issue that has garnered the attention of Arab governments. Throughout history, various Arab nations have sought to support the Palestinian cause, driven by a deep sense of solidarity and a desire to protect their regional interests. However, supporting Palestinians in their struggle for justice and self-determination presents Arab governments with a myriad of challenges, both political and practical.

1. Political Challenges

Arab governments face a complex web of political challenges when it comes to supporting the Palestinians. The interconnected nature of regional politics and international relations often forces these nations to make calculated decisions to balance their strategic interests with their support for the Palestinian cause. Key challenges include:

a) Geostrategic considerations: Arab governments often find themselves caught between the interests of their neighbouring countries and the broader international community. Maintaining diplomatic relations with Israel and appeasing influential global powers can be significant regional priorities, limiting the extent to which they can overtly support the Palestinians. For example, countries like Egypt and Jordan, which have signed peace treaties with Israel, face the challenge of striking a delicate balance between their obligations under these agreements and advocating for Palestinian rights.

Moreover, the geopolitical landscape of the Arab region plays a significant role in shaping the political challenges Arab governments face. The rivalry between regional powers, such as Saudi Arabia and Iran, further complicates matters as these nations support opposing factions within the Palestinian political landscape. Geopolitical rivalries can bifurcate Arab governments and limit the potential for a unified approach to supporting the Palestinians.

b) Arab unity and internal divisions: Despite their shared Arab identity, Arab governments have their own unique national interests and internal divisions that impact their ability to align fully in support of the Palestinians. Internal rivalries, historical disputes, and divergent political ideologies among Arab nations can hinder the coordination of a unified front in supporting the Palestinians. The fragmentation of the Arab world has weakened its collective voice and led to varying degrees of commitment to the Palestinian cause, further complicating efforts to achieve a comprehensive resolution.

Furthermore, the Arab Spring uprisings that began in 2010 and the subsequent waves of political turmoil in the region have further exacerbated internal divisions among Arab governments. The focus on domestic stability and the need to quell widespread unrest have diverted attention and resources away from active and practical support for the Palestinians.

c) Fear of retaliation: Arab governments fear the potential consequences of openly supporting the Palestinians, ranging from economic repercussions to political isolation. The fear of retaliation primarily emanates from the influence of certain global powers in the region. These powers, often driven by their interests, can exert pressure and issue threats against Arab nations that actively support the Palestinian cause. The fear of retaliation heightens the challenge of aligning their actions with their stated support for Palestinian rights, often resulting in limited or symbolic gestures rather than substantial efforts to address the underlying issues.

Furthermore, the notion of "normalisation" with Israel poses additional challenges in supporting the Palestinian cause. While some Arab countries, such as the United Arab Emirates, Bahrain, and Sudan, have recently established diplomatic relations with Israel through the Abraham Accords, others view such normalisation as a betrayal of the Palestinian cause. This divergence in approaches further complicates the unity and effectiveness of Arab governments in providing meaningful support to the Palestinians.

2. *Practical Challenges*

Beyond political obstacles, Arab governments also face practical challenges in providing meaningful support to the Palestinians:

a) Limited resources: Many Arab nations, while sympathetic to the Palestinian cause, have their own domestic and developmental priorities. More resources can be needed to ensure their ability to provide significant financial or material assistance to Palestinians in need. Economic challenges, coupled with resource constraints, make it difficult for these nations to shoulder the financial burden of supporting Palestinians effectively. The strain of refugee populations, economic stagnation, and internal conflicts further exacerbate their limitations, constraining their capacity to provide comprehensive support.

The economic challenges faced by Arab governments are multifaceted. Historically, oil-producing nations in the region, such as Saudi Arabia and Kuwait, have played a significant role in supporting the Palestinians through financial aid. However, fluctuating oil prices and economic diversification efforts have affected their ability to allocate substantial resources to the Palestinian cause. Moreover, political instability and corruption in certain Arab nations have hindered effective resource allocation, preventing the necessary support from reaching Palestinians in need.

b) Security concerns: The Israeli-Palestinian conflict often spills over into neighbouring countries, exacerbating security concerns for Arab governments. The threats posed by extremist groups, political instability, and the potential for increased violence have forced them to strike a delicate balance between maintaining national security and actively supporting the Palestinian cause. They must navigate the complexities of regional dynamics while safeguarding their stability, resulting in cautious and measured actions that may fall short of realising significant progress.

The rise of resistance groups, such as Hamas and Hezbollah, adds another layer of complexity to the security challenges faced by Arab governments supporting the Palestinians. These groups, although aligned with the Palestinian cause, may adopt tactics that undermine the stability and security of Arab rulers. Consequently, Arab governments must consider the potential consequences of their actions to prevent further destabilisation in the region.

c) Geographical barriers: Geographical proximity to Israel and Palestine presents advantages and disadvantages for Arab governments. While it enables more significant interaction and engagement, it also exposes them to direct repercussions and heightens the risk of destabilisation. The physical proximity poses logistical challenges in providing aid and support to Palestinians effectively. Additionally, border restrictions imposed by Israel further impede the flow of goods, services, and humanitarian assistance, making it arduous to address the immediate needs of Palestinians.

The geographic challenges faced by Arab governments are compounded by the historical and ongoing conflicts between Israel and its Arab neighbours. These conflicts have led to various checkpoints, barriers, and restrictions that hinder the movement of goods and people. The blockade imposed on the Gaza Strip by Israel, for instance, severely limits the ability of Arab governments to provide substantial assistance to Palestinians living in the region.

Conclusion

Arab governments face numerous challenges in supporting the Palestinians, ranging from political calculations to practical constraints. The delicate balancing act they have to perform highlights the complexities of the Israeli-Palestinian conflict and the dynamics shaping the region. Understanding and addressing these challenges is vital for fostering a comprehensive and coordinated approach to supporting the aspirations of the Palestinian people. It requires not only political will and commitment from Arab governments but also regional cooperation, international support, and resolving internal and external conflicts that impede progress. Only through concerted efforts can Arab governments play a more impactful role in advancing the rights and aspirations of the Palestinian people.

CHAPTER 20

The Global Muslim Response

The Israeli-Palestinian conflict has received widespread attention and support from the Muslim population worldwide. This chapter explores the role and impact of the global Muslim response in the quest for justice and a peaceful resolution. It will analyse the political, social, economic, cultural, and religious dimensions of Muslim support and evaluate potential consequences for Israel in a broader global context.

1. Historical and Religious Ties

Muslims, as part of the broader Abrahamic faith tradition, have significant historical and religious ties to the land of Palestine. The Al-Aqsa Mosque in Jerusalem, one of the holiest sites in Islam, holds immense spiritual significance for Muslims worldwide. This deep connection has fuelled the solidarity and support shown by Muslims for the Palestinian cause. The historical narrative of Muslims regarding the land of Palestine, including the establishment of various Muslim empires, such as the Umayyad, Abbasid, and Ottoman empires, further strengthens their emotional and religious attachment to the cause.

2. Political Support

Numerous Muslim-majority countries, such as Egypt, Jordan, Turkey, Iran, Indonesia, Malaysia, and Pakistan, have consistently expressed support for the Palestinian people and their struggle for self-determination. Diplomatic efforts, including sending aid, lobbying for international resolutions, and offering political asylum, are all part of the global Muslim response. These nations often leverage their political and economic influence, along with their membership in regional organisations like the Organisation of Islamic Cooperation (OIC), to raise awareness and advocate for the rights of Palestinians. Some countries, such as Iran, have even gone as far as questioning the legitimacy of Israel's existence, leading to strained diplomatic relations.

3. Civil Society Mobilisation

Muslim communities worldwide, both individuals and organisations, play an essential role in supporting the Palestinian cause. Grassroots movements, like the Boycott, Divestment, and Sanctions (BDS) movement, fundraising campaigns, and demonstrations serve as vehicles for expressing solidarity and raising awareness about the plight of Palestinians. These efforts aim to pressure governments, international institutions, and corporations to change policies and support the Palestinian cause. The Palestinian diaspora and Palestinian solidarity organisations also contribute to this mobilisation, actively advocating on various platforms for the rights and recognition of Palestinians.

4. Economic Assistance

Muslim-majority countries and organisations have also provided significant economic assistance to the Palestinian territories. Financial aid, investments, and development projects contribute to infrastructure development, healthcare, education, and other essential services. These initiatives aim to empower Palestinians and alleviate their socioeconomic hardships, fostering hope for a better future. Countries like Saudi Arabia, Qatar, Kuwait, Turkey, and the United Arab Emirates have created funds specifically dedicated to supporting Palestinian causes, emphasising the importance of collective responsibility in providing for those affected by the conflict.

5. Media and Information Dissemination

Muslim media outlets, both traditional and digital, have played and continue to play a crucial role in disseminating information and shaping public perceptions about the Israeli-Palestinian conflict. These platforms highlight the experiences and narratives of Palestinians, amplifying their voices and countering biased narratives. Social media campaigns, documentaries, and journalistic work are critical components of this effort to raise global awareness. Muslim influencers and activists engage with audiences worldwide, utilising social media platforms to share real-time updates, personal stories, and images from the ground, thus generating empathy and support.

6. Cultural and Interfaith Initiatives

Muslim communities, recognising the significance of cultural and interfaith dialogue, have actively engaged in initiatives promoting understanding and cooperation. Interfaith dialogues, conferences, and educational programmes aim to bridge gaps, challenge stereotypes, and foster empathy among religious communities. Muslim artists, writers, and filmmakers have also utilised their creative platforms to tell the story behind the conflict, invoking emotions and promoting understanding among diverse audiences. These cultural initiatives humanise the Palestinian narrative and promote empathy and understanding, ultimately contributing to the global Muslim response.

7. The Impact on Israel

The global Muslim response exerts significant pressure on Israel, both politically and economically. International recognition of Palestine as a state, divestment campaigns, and boycott movements challenge Israel's policies and actions. Moreover, the Muslim response underscores the notion that the continued occupation, human rights abuses, and lack of a just resolution to the conflict violate accepted principles of international law and human rights norms. Israel's relationships with various Muslim-majority countries have faced strain, affecting diplomatic efforts and regional dynamics. The growing global Muslim response puts pressure on Israel to reconsider its approach and engage in meaningful dialogues for a resolution that respects the rights and aspirations of both Palestinians and Israelis.

Conclusion

The extended global Muslim response to the Israeli-Palestinian conflict demonstrates the widespread support and solidarity offered to the Palestinian people by Muslims worldwide. This response's political, social, economic, cultural, and religious dimensions play a pivotal role in raising awareness, exerting pressure, and advocating for a just and lasting peace. The international support provided by the Muslim community contributes to a broader global dialogue. It underscores the importance of finding a fair resolution to the Israeli-Palestinian conflict for regional stability and justice. By engaging in diplomatic efforts, media campaigns, cultural initiatives, and economic assistance, Muslims assert their commitment to justice, human rights, and self-determination for all people, regardless of their religious or ethnic backgrounds. This global solidarity challenges the status quo and calls for a comprehensive and inclusive resolution that respects the rights and aspirations of both Palestinians and Israelis, ultimately contributing to a more peaceful and just world.

CHAPTER 21

Analysis of the Support Received by Palestinians From the Muslim Population Worldwide

The Israeli-Palestinian conflict has sparked a vast and diverse array of responses from the global Muslim community. This chapter delves into the multifaceted support Palestinians receive from Muslims worldwide. Analysing this solidarity's political, social, and economic dimensions demonstrates the depth and significance of Muslim support and its potential implications for the Israeli-Palestinian conflict.

1. The Roots of Muslim Support

1.1 Historical Perspective:
Muslim support for the Palestinian cause is deeply rooted in history. The significance of Jerusalem and the revered Al-Aqsa Mosque, as well as the rich Arab-Islamic heritage of the region, have struck a chord with Muslims worldwide. Dating back to the early days of the conflict,

the liberation of Palestine has become a common cause, reflecting both religious devotion and emotional attachment to the land and a desire to protect sacred sites from encroachment.

1.2 The Role of Islamic Organisations:
Islamic organisations play a pivotal role in mobilising support for Palestinians. From well-established non-governmental organisations to grassroots religious movements, these groups emphasise the importance of backing Palestinian self-determination and resilience against occupation. They raise global awareness about the plight of Palestinians and advocate for their rights through various means, such as organising conferences, providing legal aid, coordinating humanitarian relief efforts, and engaging in cultural and educational programmes.

2. Political Dimensions of Muslim Support

2.1 Diplomatic Efforts:
Muslim-majority countries consistently voice their support for the Palestinian cause on international platforms. They leverage their positions to promote Palestinian rights, denounce Israeli occupation and aggression, and advocate for a just solution to the conflict. This solidarity helps maintain global attention on the Palestinian issue and sustains pressure on Israel. Nations like Malaysia, Indonesia, Turkey, and Iran spearhead initiatives, raising awareness about the Palestinian struggle and pushing for tangible resolutions.

2.2 Financial Assistance

Besides political support, many Muslim countries provide financial aid to Palestinians, including individuals and institutions, to mitigate the economic hardships caused by occupation and conflict. This support includes direct donations, contributions to development projects, and investments in sectors crucial to Palestinian livelihoods, such as healthcare, education, and infrastructure. Moreover, Muslim communities and individuals worldwide engage actively in charitable efforts, donating funds for medical facilities, orphanages, schools, and other essential services.

3. Social and Cultural Dimensions of Muslim Support

3.1 Grassroots Movements:

Muslims outside the conflict zone, through grassroots movements and initiatives, actively participate in promoting the Palestinian cause. They organise protests, demonstrations, and educational campaigns to raise awareness about the struggle and the injustices faced by Palestinians. These efforts highlight the power of public sentiment, creating platforms for individuals to express their support for Palestinians and demand justice. The Boycott, Divestment, and Sanctions (BDS) movement, led by various Muslim and non-Muslim activists, has gained significant traction, urging individuals and organisations to boycott Israeli goods and businesses complicit in the occupation.

3.2 Humanitarian Support:

Muslim individuals and organisations are at the forefront of providing humanitarian assistance to Palestinians affected by the conflict. Medical aid, food, shelter, and educational programmes offered by these groups help alleviate the suffering caused by the occupation, blockades, and recurrent military campaigns. Humanitarian organisations like Islamic Relief, Qatar Charity, and various local Muslim charities work tirelessly to address the urgent needs of Palestinians, nurturing hope and resilience in the face of adversity.

4. Implications of Muslim Support

4.1 Strengthening Palestinian Identity:
Muslim support reinforces the collective identity of Palestinians. By demonstrating their solidarity, Muslims worldwide provide a sense of unity and a reminder that Palestinians are not alone in their struggle for justice and self-determination. Cultural exchanges, academic scholarships, and artistic collaborations initiated by Muslim organisations help promote Palestinian culture and heritage, ensuring its preservation amidst ongoing challenges.

4.2 International Pressure:
The global Muslim response to the Israeli-Palestinian conflict adds an additional layer of support for Palestinians. This collective solidarity, combined with diplomatic efforts, international resolutions, and public opinion, exerts pressure on relevant governments and international actors involved in the conflict. The unified voice of the global Muslim community serves as a constant reminder that the Israeli-Palestinian conflict is not isolated but carries broader implications for regional stability, justice, and human rights.

4.3 Bridging Divides and Encouraging Dialogue:
Muslim support for Palestinians also opens avenues for interfaith and intercultural dialogue. It encourages partnerships with Jewish and Christian communities that advocate for peace and justice in the region. These dialogues foster understanding, shift perceptions, and explore shared values, leading to a more inclusive narrative that transcends religious boundaries and seeks a comprehensive resolution to the conflict.

Conclusion

The global Muslim response to the Israeli-Palestinian conflict encompasses political, social, and economic dimensions of support. Muslim individuals, organisations, and governments express their unwavering solidarity with Palestinians, emphasising the significance of the Palestinian cause within the broader context of the Muslim community's collective aspirations for justice, human rights, and self-determination. This comprehensive support not only strengthens the Palestinian identity and resilience but also adds significant pressure on international actors to pursue a just and lasting resolution to the conflict. The global Muslim response serves as a testament to the unwavering commitment of Muslims worldwide to stand with the Palestinians, fostering hope and pushing for a future of peace and dignity for all.

CHAPTER 22

Examination of the Political, Social, and Economic Dimensions of Muslim Support

The Israeli-Palestinian conflict is not merely a localised issue; it has garnered significant attention and support from Muslim communities around the world. Understanding the multifaceted dimensions of Muslim support for the Palestinian cause is crucial in comprehending the full extent of this conflict.

1. Political Dimension

Within the political sphere, Muslim support for the Palestinians materialises through diplomatic efforts and solidarity expressed by Muslim-majority countries. Many nations have voiced their unwavering support for Palestinian statehood and self-determination. These countries often reiterate the importance of upholding international law and resolutions about the conflict, emphasising the need for a just and comprehensive peace agreement between Israel and Palestine.

Turkey has been at the forefront of Muslim nations advocating for the Palestinian cause. Building upon historical ties between Turkey and the Arab world, the Turkish government has actively engaged in diplomatic initiatives to promote Palestinian rights and advocate for a two-state solution. Turkey has not only provided political support but also financial backing to various Palestinian development projects, demonstrating its commitment to building a sustainable future for the Palestinians.

Egypt, as another influential regional player, has played a pivotal role in mediating negotiations between Israel and Palestine. Through its diplomatic efforts, Egypt has sought to facilitate dialogue and push for a peaceful resolution to the longstanding conflict. Its geographical proximity to Gaza has amplified its responsibility in providing humanitarian aid and relief to Palestinians in the besieged territory.

Iran, although geographically distant from the conflict, has consistently voiced its solidarity with the Palestinian cause. As a Shia-majority country, Iran presents itself as the protector of Muslim interests, thereby taking a strong stance against Israeli policies and supporting armed resistance groups. Iran's support for Hamas and Islamic Jihad serves as a form of military and political backing, subject to its broader geopolitical considerations in the region.

The Organisation of Islamic Cooperation (OIC) serves as a collective voice for Muslim nations on global issues, including the Israeli-Palestinian conflict. Comprising 57 Muslim-majority countries, the OIC regularly convenes meetings and sends delegations to international forums to raise awareness about the Palestinian cause and garner support for their demands. The OIC resolutions and statements carry weight in the international arena, urging member states to take concrete action and influence global policies.

Furthermore, Muslim leaders and organisations frequently advocate for the rights of Palestinians in various international forums, such as the United Nations. These platforms serve as channels to raise awareness about the Palestinian plight and pressure the international community to take action. By maintaining a visible stance on this issue, Muslim nations exert political influence and contribute to shaping the global narrative surrounding the conflict.

2. Social Dimension

At the grassroots level, Muslim support for the Palestinians is evident in the solidarity expressed by individuals, communities, and organisations. Muslims worldwide engage in various forms of activism, including protests, boycotts, and awareness campaigns to highlight the suffering and injustices faced by Palestinians. These efforts aim to raise public awareness, mobilise support, and hold accountable entities complicit in perpetuating the conflict.

Social media platforms have played a significant role in mobilising support, enabling individuals to share stories, images, and videos that shed light on the Palestinian experience. Hashtags such as #FreePalestine and #SaveSheikhJarrah have trended globally, amplifying the voices of Palestinians and their supporters. These digital platforms also allow for the dissemination of information, facilitating global conversations about the root causes and potential solutions to the conflict.

Moreover, religious ties between Muslims and Palestine contribute to a strong sense of kinship and empathy. The Al-Aqsa Mosque, the third holiest site in Islam, holds profound religious and symbolic significance for Muslims. The collective attachment to this sacred place strengthens the emotional connection between Muslims and the Palestinian cause. This sentiment is further fuelled by historical and religious narratives that emphasise the importance of Jerusalem in Islamic history.

Muslim scholars and religious leaders have also played a significant role in mobilising support for the Palestinians. They utilise religious teachings and principles to highlight the moral and ethical imperatives of standing with the oppressed and seeking justice. Their sermons, lectures, and writings often invoke Islamic values of compassion, justice, and solidarity to galvanise support and inspire activism.

Interfaith dialogue and cooperation have also been instrumental in promoting a broader understanding of the Israeli-Palestinian conflict. Muslim interfaith organisations collaborate with individuals from various religious backgrounds to foster mutual understanding and work towards a peaceful resolution.

3. Economic Dimension

Muslim support for Palestine extends to the economic realm as well. Muslim-majority countries often provide financial aid and development assistance to support the Palestinian people. These contributions are channelled towards healthcare, education, infrastructure, and rebuilding efforts in the conflict-affected areas.

The Kingdom of Saudi Arabia, a long-time supporter of Palestinian causes, has significantly contributed to Palestinian development projects, funding various initiatives and providing substantial aid. Its financial assistance encompasses many areas, including education, healthcare, and infrastructure. The Saudi Fund for Development and King Salman

Humanitarian Aid and Relief Centre has actively supported Palestinian institutions and assisted in post-conflict reconstruction efforts.

Qatar has similarly supported Palestinian reconstruction efforts through its Qatar Fund for Development. It has focused on infrastructure, housing, and healthcare facilities to enhance living conditions and provide essential services to Palestinians. Qatar's economic support also extends to its investments in Palestinian businesses and industries, aiming to boost the Palestinian economy and create sustainable growth opportunities.

In addition to government contributions, Muslim individuals and organisations worldwide have established charitable initiatives and campaigns to provide humanitarian aid to Palestinians in need. These initiatives range from providing food, shelter, and healthcare assistance to funding young Palestinians' education and vocational training programmes. These efforts aim to alleviate immediate suffering and empower Palestinian communities to build sustainable futures.

Moreover, Muslim businesses play a role in supporting Palestine by engaging in fair trade practices and promoting Palestinian products in global markets. By sourcing goods from Palestinian farmers and enterprises, Muslim entrepreneurs not only contribute to the Palestinian economy but also raise awareness about the struggles faced by local producers under occupation. These efforts provide economic support and aim to empower Palestinian communities by creating sustainable livelihood opportunities.

In conclusion, the political, social, and economic dimensions of Muslim support for the Palestinian cause are interwoven and deeply interconnected. The solidarity expressed by Muslim-majority nations and individuals reflects a shared commitment to justice, freedom, and self-determination. Through diplomatic efforts, social activism, and economic assistance, Muslims worldwide contribute to shaping the discourse surrounding the Israeli-Palestinian conflict and advocate for a fair and lasting resolution. Recognising these dimensions is vital in understanding the global response to the plight of the Palestinians and the potential for cultivating a just and peaceful future for all parties involved.

CHAPTER 23

Evaluation of the Potential Consequences For Israel in a Broader Global Context

In this chapter, we will critically assess the potential consequences Israel may face in the context of a broader global setting. By examining the intricate dynamics between Israel and the international community, we aim to provide an objective analysis of the various consequences that may arise due to the Israeli-Palestinian conflict.

1. Diplomatic Isolation: A Growing Concern

One of Israel's most significant potential consequences is the risk of diplomatic isolation. As the conflict continues, concern over Israel's policies and actions in the occupied territories grows among the international community. Countries and international organisations increasingly voice their objections and express grave concerns, leading to strained diplomatic relations and potential sanctions.

Israel's strong ties with the United States have traditionally provided a buffer against complete isolation. However, evolving dynamics within the international arena, changing alliances, and shifting global power dynamics may weaken this support over time. As countries seek to align themselves with emerging global powers or pursue their own agendas, they may reassess their relationships with Israel, potentially isolating it diplomatically.

Furthermore, the United Nations and its various bodies, such as the General Assembly and Human Rights Council, have played a significant role in amplifying criticism of Israel's actions. The frequent resolutions condemning Israel, particularly regarding settlement expansion and occupation, create a perception among some that Israel consistently disregards international opinion and diplomatic norms.

2. Damage to International Reputation

Israel's actions in the conflict have often been heavily scrutinised, leading to damage to its international reputation. The use of disproportionate force, controversial policies, and allegations of human rights violations have drawn criticism and condemnation from various nations and human rights organisations. Such negative perceptions can impact Israel's standing in the global arena, influencing trade, tourism, and foreign investment.

Critics argue that Israel's policies and actions, particularly in the occupied territories, contravene international law and violate the principles of human rights. Instances such as the demolition of Palestinian homes, restrictive movement controls, the expansion of settlements, and the blockade on Gaza have garnered widespread condemnation, creating a perception that Israel is disregarding international norms.

This damaged reputation not only affects political and diplomatic relations but also has indirect economic consequences. Tourism, a significant sector in Israel, may suffer from boycott calls and decreased interest from potential visitors concerned about the human rights situation. Furthermore, foreign investment decisions may be influenced by ethical considerations, leading some companies and investors to hesitate or completely avoid engaging with Israeli businesses.

Moreover, the increasing use of social media platforms and the proliferation of information sources have allowed for the rapid dissemination and amplification of contentious incidents related to the Israeli-Palestinian conflict. Images and videos portraying the suffering of individuals caught in the crossfire have garnered global attention, contributing to negative perceptions of Israel's policies and actions.

3. Impact on Regional Stability

The Israeli-Palestinian conflict has broader implications for regional stability in the Middle East. Continued tensions and violence in the region can lead to a ripple effect, exacerbating conflicts and contributing to regional instability. This, in turn, may disrupt regional cooperation, compromise peace agreements, and give rise to extremism and radicalisation, posing a threat to Israel and neighbouring countries.

The Middle East is a complex web of interrelated conflicts and competing interests. The unresolved Israeli-Palestinian conflict is often viewed as a key destabilising factor in the region. The perpetuation of this conflict serves as fuel for extremists who exploit the grievances of Palestinians and anti-Israel sentiment to advance their own agendas. The rise of extremist groups, such as Hamas or Hezbollah, and their ability to gain support and recruits are partially tied to the unresolved conflict.

Moreover, the polarisation resulting from the Israeli-Palestinian conflict has strained relationships between Israel and some Arab states. While the Abraham Accords offer a glimmer of hope for increased regional cooperation, the deep-rooted sentiments surrounding the Israeli-Palestinian issue continue to shape regional dynamics.

The potential consequences of regional instability extend beyond immediate security concerns. Economic cooperation and integration, essential for regional development, suffer when conflicts persist. The lack of trust and political will hinders efforts to forge economic ties and mutually beneficial partnerships, limiting Israel's potential for regional economic growth and prosperity.

4. Economic Consequences

The enduring conflict adversely affects the economy of the entire region, including Israel. Repeated military operations and ongoing security measures divert significant resources towards defence and security, leaving less for economic development and social welfare. Furthermore, a lack of stability and trust hinders foreign investment, impeding economic growth and potentially leading to economic decline.

The conflict imposes significant economic burdens on Israel. Defence expenditures consume a considerable portion of the national budget, diverting funds away from infrastructure development, healthcare, education, and social welfare programmes. The constant threat of violence and the need for security measures hamper economic productivity and diminish the country's potential for growth.

Israel's regional trade is also affected by the conflict. The absence of normalised commercial relations with neighbouring Arab states and, to some extent, other Muslim-majority countries hampers opportunities for trade, investment, and economic cooperation. These missed economic opportunities hinder Israel's potential for long-term prosperity.

Additionally, the conflict creates a volatile environment that inhibits entrepreneurial activities and discourages foreign companies from investing in Israel. The uncertainty surrounding the conflict and the potential for violence pose significant risks for businesses, potentially deterring potential investors and hindering economic development.

Furthermore, the economic consequences extend beyond Israel's borders. The economic interdependence of the region means that economic shocks in one country can have ripple effects throughout the region. Any economic deterioration in Israel can reverberate across neighbouring economies, potentially exacerbating existing economic challenges.

5. Cultural and Academic Boycotts

Another potential consequence for Israel lies in the growing movement for cultural and academic boycotts. Artists, academics, and organisations increasingly choose to abstain from engaging with Israeli institutions and individuals due to their complicity, real or perceived, in the occupation and other contentious policies. Academic collaborations, cultural exchanges, and international events may be affected, limiting Israel's participation and hindering intellectual growth and diversity.

The Boycott, Divestment, and Sanctions (BDS) movement, which advocates for various forms of boycott against Israel, has gained traction in several countries and on university campuses. While responses to the BDS movement vary across countries and institutions, its influence cannot be ignored. Supporters argue that cultural and academic boycotts are nonviolent means to pressure Israel into addressing the conflict. Critics, on the other hand, argue that such boycotts hinder dialogue and understanding, perpetuating divisions and preventing opportunities for mutual understanding and peacebuilding.

These cultural and academic boycotts can impact Israel's academic and cultural institutions, limiting their global reach and hindering collaboration with international counterparts. The exchange of ideas, research partnerships, and artistic collaborations may be curtailed, denying the Israeli intellectual community opportunities for growth and potential breakthroughs.

In response to cultural and academic boycotts, Israel has sought to counteract these efforts through various means. It has invested in presenting its national narrative, supporting pro-Israel organisations and initiatives, and encouraging dialogue to counter the negative portrayal of its policies. Nonetheless, the growing prevalence of boycotts presents an ongoing challenge to Israel's aspirations for academic and cultural engagement.

6. Perception of Impediments to Peace

Israel's position and actions in the conflict have raised concerns about its commitment to achieving a peaceful resolution. This perception has consequences in terms of international support for peace efforts and the potential for future negotiations.

Critics argue that Israel's continued expansion of settlements in the occupied territories and the lack of progress in resolving the core issues of the conflict create an image of an unwillingness to compromise. This perception can undermine international support for Israel's position and make it more challenging to garner backing for peace initiatives.

Moreover, the continuation of the conflict and the lack of progress towards a resolution undermine the viability of the two-state solution. As time goes on and settlements expand, the prospects for a contiguous and viable Palestinian state diminish, raising concerns about the long-term prospects for peace in the region.

The perception that Israel is impeding progress towards a peaceful resolution also impacts the Palestinian leadership's position. If the international community believes that Israel is not acting in good faith, it may be less inclined to pressure the Palestinian Authority to make concessions or engage in negotiations.

7. *Potential for Escalation and Escalation of Conflict*

The Israeli-Palestinian conflict is characterised by cycles of violence and retaliation, with the potential for further escalation always looming. The consequences of further escalation are significant and potentially catastrophic.

Escalation in the conflict could lead to a full-scale war involving neighbouring countries. Arab states that are already critical of Israel's policies may seize the opportunity to challenge and confront Israel militarily. This, in turn, would trigger a range of potential consequences, from regional instability to civilian casualties and humanitarian crises.

Furthermore, escalating violence can spark acts of terrorism and retaliatory attacks, not only within the region but also globally. Terrorist groups like Hamas and Hezbollah have previously launched attacks outside the conflict zone, targeting Israeli interests or Jewish communities elsewhere in the world. Escalation could reignite such acts of violence, compromising international security.

Another consequence of escalation is the potential use of weapons of mass destruction. Given the regional tensions and existing arms race in the Middle East, any escalation could heighten the risk of the use of chemical, biological, or nuclear weapons. The consequences of such a scenario would be catastrophic, not only for the region but also for global security and stability.

Conclusion: Navigating the Complex Consequences

Examining the potential consequences of the Israeli-Palestinian conflict within a broader global context reveals the intricate dynamics and challenges that Israel faces. From diplomatic isolation to economic consequences, damaged reputation, and the potential for escalation, Israel must navigate a complex landscape to secure its long-term peace and prosperity.

Addressing these potential consequences requires a multifaceted approach that considers all stakeholders' interests and concerns. This includes fostering dialogue and negotiations to advance the peace process, addressing humanitarian concerns, and creating an environment conducive to economic development and regional cooperation.

Ultimately, sustainable peace and stability in the region require a commitment from all parties involved. It necessitates a willingness to seek common ground, engage in dialogue, and make difficult compromises. Only through a collective effort can the potential consequences be mitigated and a future of peace and prosperity for Israel and the region be realised.

CHAPTER 24

Attempts at Peace and Their Failures

Throughout the Israeli-Palestinian conflict, numerous attempts have been made to bring about a peaceful resolution. This chapter delves into the history of these endeavours, shedding light on the reasons behind their failures and the persistent obstacles hindering a lasting peace agreement.

1. PREVIOUS PEACE INITIATIVES

1.1 Oslo Accords (1993):

- Overview of the Oslo Accords and its significance as a framework for peace.
- Analysis of the key agreements reached between Israel and the Palestinian Liberation Organisation (PLO).
- Examination of the challenges encountered during the implementation phase.
- Detailed exploration of the core issues discussed, including borders, settlements, security, Jerusalem, and the right of return.
- Discussion on the impact of the assassination of Israeli Prime Minister Yitzhak Rabin on the peace process.

1.2 Camp David Summit (2000):

- Evaluation of the negotiations at the Camp David Summit facilitated by the United States.

- Discussion on contentious issues, including borders, Jerusalem, settlements, refugees, and security.

- Analysis of the factors contributing to the collapse of the summit and the subsequent outbreak of violence.

- In-depth examination of the role and positions of both Israeli Prime Minister Ehud Barak and Palestinian Authority Chairman Yasser Arafat.

- Exploration of missed opportunities and the potential breakthroughs that could have altered the course of negotiations.

1.3 Annapolis Conference (2007):

- Exploration of the Annapolis Conference and its attempt to revive negotiations.

- Assessment of the role of regional and international actors in the conference's outcomes.

- Evaluation of the challenges faced in implementing the agreements made during the conference.

- Analysis of the Quartet's efforts (comprised of the United States, European Union, United Nations, and Russia) to facilitate peace.

- Discussion on the role of economic development as a component of peace and the failure to address economic disparities during these negotiations.

2. OBSTACLES TO PEACE

2.1 Israeli Settlements:

- Analysis of the impact and growth of Israeli settlements in the occupied territories.

- Examination of the legal implications and the challenges settlements pose to a two-state solution.

- Discussion on the Israeli government's stance towards settlements and its implications on peace efforts.
- In-depth exploration of settlement-related issues such as construction, expansion, and the eviction of Palestinian residents.
- Evaluation of the impact of settlement building on the trust and confidence needed for successful negotiations.

2.2 Security Concerns:
- Evaluation of Israel's security concerns and their influence on peace negotiations.
- Analysis of the difficulties in reconciling Israeli security needs and Palestinian aspirations.
- Exploration of potential mechanisms to address these security concerns while ensuring Palestinian rights.
- Examination of the impact of violence and terrorism on Israeli security concerns and its effect on peace talks.
- Discussion on the importance of building mutual trust and security cooperation between both parties.

2.3 Palestinian Political Division:
- Assessment of the internal divisions within the Palestinian leadership and society.
- Exploration of the impact of the Fatah-Hamas divide on peace negotiations.
- Discussion on the efforts to reconcile the factions and the implications for future peace efforts.
- Analysis of the Palestinian Authority's governance challenges and its impact on unity and negotiations.
- Examination of the significance of democratic representation and inclusivity in Palestinian decision-making processes.

3. REGIONAL AND INTERNATIONAL INFLUENCES

3.1 Role of Arab States:

- Analysis of the role played by various Arab states in facilitating or hindering peace efforts.
- Examination of the Arab Peace Initiative and its potential impact on the conflict.
- Discussion on the challenges Arab states face in maintaining a unified stance towards the Israeli-Palestinian conflict.
- Evaluation of regional support for Palestinian autonomy and the Arab states' approach to normalising relations with Israel.
- Exploration of historical and geopolitical factors influencing Arab engagement in the peace process.

3.2 International Mediation:

- Evaluation of the effectiveness of international mediation efforts, including those led by the United States, the European Union, and the United Nations.
- Analysis of the limitations and biases in these mediation processes.
- Exploration of potential ways to enhance international mediation for better peace prospects.
- In-depth examination of the role and impact of regional and international actors in shaping peace negotiations.
- Discussion on the need for inclusion of diverse perspectives and more concerted efforts from the international community to ensure a fair and unbiased mediation process.

Conclusion

Despite multiple attempts at peace, the Israeli-Palestinian conflict remains unresolved. The failures of previous peace initiatives can be attributed to a multitude of factors, including contentious issues, divergent security concerns, internal political divisions, settlement expansion, and external influences. Overcoming these obstacles and achieving a lasting peace will require the dedication and participation of all relevant parties, as well as international support and the willingness to compromise. To move forward, a comprehensive understanding of these failures is critical in charting a new, inclusive, and equitable path towards a peaceful and just resolution to the Israeli-Palestinian conflict.

CHAPTER 25

Overview of Previous Peace Initiatives and Negotiations

In the turbulent history of the Israeli-Palestinian conflict, numerous attempts have been made to achieve a peaceful resolution that addresses the legitimate aspirations of both parties. These initiatives and negotiations have aimed to find a comprehensive solution to the complex issues at hand. This chapter provides an in-depth overview of some of the key peace initiatives and negotiations that have taken place, highlighting their strengths, weaknesses, and ultimate failures.

1. Oslo Accords (1993-1995)

One of the most significant peace initiatives in the history of the conflict, the Oslo Accords marked the first direct negotiations between Israel and the Palestine Liberation Organisation (PLO). The Accords aimed to establish self-governance for Palestinians in the occupied territories, leading to the creation of the Palestinian Authority. Under the Oslo process, the Palestinians were to gain control over civil matters in specified areas, while the status of Jerusalem, final borders, and the fate of Israeli settlements were to be negotiated in subsequent phases.

Despite its initial promise, the Oslo process faced numerous obstacles, including territorial disputes, settlement expansions, and continued acts of violence. These challenges eventually led to its eventual breakdown and failure to achieve a lasting peace. The assassination of Israeli Prime Minister Yitzhak Rabin, a key advocate for the peace process, further diminished the chances of its successful implementation.

Critics argue that the Oslo process lacked clear parameters, leading to its ambiguity and protracted nature. There was no agreed-upon deadline for the establishment of a Palestinian state, leaving room for indefinite delays and stalling tactics by both parties. Moreover, the failure to address key issues, such as the status of Jerusalem and the right of return for Palestinian refugees, also contributed to the collapse of the Oslo process. The subsequent failure to implement agreed-upon provisions and the escalating violence in the aftermath further strained relations between Israelis and Palestinians, casting a shadow of doubt on the viability of future negotiations.

2. Camp David Summit (2000)

Under the leadership of then-Israeli Prime Minister Ehud Barak and President Bill Clinton's involvement, the Camp David Summit aimed to resolve the final status issues of the Israeli-Palestinian conflict. This summit represented a historic moment, where the leaders came together to negotiate and address crucial issues such as borders, settlements, Jerusalem, and the right of return for Palestinian refugees.

However, the summit failed, underscoring the wide gaps that existed between the two sides. The final settlement proposals put forward by

Barak were seen as insufficient by the Palestinians, who believed their legitimate rights and aspirations had not been adequately addressed.

Critics argue that the timing and dynamics surrounding the Camp David Summit significantly affected its failure. The summit took place amidst rising tensions and violence, with the Second Intifada erupting shortly after its collapse. Israeli settlements continued to expand and solidify their presence in the occupied territories, making a future contiguous Palestinian state increasingly unlikely. The inability to reach a mutually accepted resolution on Jerusalem, a city of immense religious and national significance for both parties, further complicated the negotiations. The collapse of the summit reverberated throughout the region, pushing both Israelis and Palestinians into a protracted cycle of violence and further undermining trust and confidence in the peace process.

3. Arab Peace Initiative (2002)

Proposed by the Arab League, the Arab Peace Initiative offered Israel full peace and diplomatic relations in exchange for withdrawing from territories occupied since 1967 and the establishment of a viable and sovereign Palestinian state. This initiative aimed to address the broader regional context of the Israeli-Palestinian conflict by involving Arab states. It was a significant step towards regional normalisation and offered a potential path for Israel's integration into the Middle East.

However, despite its noble intentions, the Israeli government rejected the initiative, raising concerns over its specific stipulations and the question of refugees. Israeli leaders argued that the Arab Peace Initiative did not address the complexities surrounding the right of return for Palestinian refugees and did not provide sufficient guarantees for Israel's security.

Critics note that while the Arab Peace Initiative provided a promising framework for regional peace, the rejection from the Israeli side highlighted the difficulty in finding consensus on the most contentious issues. Additionally, some critics argue that the initiative did not fully acknowledge Israeli concerns regarding security and the regional balance of power. Despite its rejection, the Arab Peace Initiative remains a compelling example of the region's desire for a comprehensive and just resolution.

4. Annapolis Conference (2007)

Under the auspices of President George W. Bush, the Annapolis Conference sought to jumpstart peace negotiations between Israel and the Palestinians. It aimed to address the core issues of the conflict, such as borders, settlements, the status of Jerusalem, and the right of return for Palestinian refugees.

The conference brought together Israeli Prime Minister Ehud Olmert and Palestinian President Mahmoud Abbas, with the active involvement of international mediators. Despite an initial framework agreement being reached outlining potential solutions to key issues, the talks ultimately collapsed, and mistrust between the parties deepened.

Critics argue that the Annapolis Conference faced significant obstacles, including internal political dynamics and rising violence on the ground. For the Israeli side, the ongoing expansion of settlements in the occupied territories eroded trust and confidence in the peace process. On the Palestinian side, the deep divisions between the Fatah-led Palestinian Authority and Hamas, which controlled the Gaza Strip, further complicated negotiations. Ultimately, the inability to translate the initial framework agreement into tangible progress eroded hope and undermined the impetus for further negotiations.

5. John Kerry's Peace Initiative (2013-2014)

United States Secretary of State, John Kerry, invested significant efforts in a peace initiative, engaging directly with Israeli and Palestinian leadership. Recognising the urgent need for a resolution, Kerry embarked on an intense round of shuttle diplomacy, attempting to bridge the gaps between the two sides.

The negotiations faced various hurdles, including settlement expansions, continued violence, and deep-seated mistrust. Although a framework agreement was proposed outlining potential solutions to key issues, the talks ultimately collapsed, and mistrust between the parties deepened.

Critics argue that the collapse of the Kerry-led initiative highlighted the challenge of sustaining commitment from both parties. Israeli settlements continued to expand, making a contiguous Palestinian state increasingly challenging to achieve. Palestinian frustration grew as they perceived a lack of genuine commitment from Israel to fulfil its obligations and address their core concerns. The broader regional and geopolitical factors also played a role, with the increasingly polarised dynamics in the Middle East further complicating the prospects for a comprehensive peace agreement.

Conclusion

Despite the sincere efforts and considerable resources expended in previous peace initiatives and negotiations, a comprehensive and lasting resolution to the Israeli-Palestinian conflict remains elusive. These initiatives have revealed the complexities, deep-rooted issues, and mistrust that exist between the parties.

The historical context, territorial disputes, security concerns, the status of Jerusalem, the right of return for Palestinian refugees, and the question of Israeli settlements have all contributed to the failures of these peace initiatives. Moreover, internal political factors, regional dynamics, and the influence of extremist groups have further complicated the path to peace.

Nonetheless, these previous attempts provide valuable lessons and insights that may inform future peace processes. It is essential for all parties involved to reflect upon these experiences, learn from their shortcomings, and recommit to a just, equitable, and inclusive path of negotiations.

Moving forward, addressing the key issues that have hindered progress in previous peace initiatives is crucial. The status of Jerusalem, a city of immense religious and national significance for both Israelis and Palestinians, must be approached with sensitivity and creative solutions that respect the aspirations and rights of both parties. The question of settlements, which have expanded and solidified their presence in the occupied territories, needs to be addressed in a fair and equitable manner that respects international law and the rights of Palestinians.

The right of return for Palestinian refugees, a deeply emotional and complex issue, necessitates a comprehensive solution that recognises the suffering and displacement experienced by Palestinians while also respecting the demographic and security concerns of Israel. Finding a balance that acknowledges the legitimate aspirations of both parties and provides redress for past injustices is crucial for any future agreement.

Internal divisions within both the Israeli and Palestinian leadership have hampered progress in previous negotiations. It is essential for both sides to foster unity and create a unified front to negotiate effectively and implement any potential agreements. A shared vision and purpose will build trust, credibility, and a sense of ownership in the peace process.

The involvement of regional and international actors is crucial in creating an enabling environment for negotiations. Arab states and the broader international community can play a significant role in supporting and facilitating negotiations, providing incentives, and ensuring the implementation of any agreements reached.

Future peace initiatives must also learn from past mistakes and ensure a clear timeline, defined parameters, and a transparent framework for negotiations. The lack of clarity and ambiguity surrounding previous peace processes contributed to their collapse and the erosion of trust between the parties. Establishing clear guidelines and deadlines will help maintain momentum and prevent indefinite delays and stalling tactics.

Ultimately, achieving a comprehensive and lasting peace between Israelis and Palestinians requires a genuine commitment and political will from both sides. It necessitates a recognition of the legitimate rights and aspirations of both parties and a willingness to make difficult compromises for the sake of peace and a better future for generations to come.

While the road to peace may be challenging, the shared desire for security, stability, and prosperity provides a foundation for progress. By learning from the lessons of the past and approaching negotiations with creativity, empathy, and determination, a just and lasting resolution to the Israeli-Palestinian conflict may become within reach if Israel and its Western supporters are serious about the two states' solution.

CHAPTER 26

Exploration of the Obstacles and Failures in Achieving a Lasting Peace

The search for a lasting peace between Israel and Palestine has been a long and arduous journey, filled with numerous obstacles and failures. Despite the aspirations and efforts of many individuals and organisations, reaching a resolution that satisfies both sides has remained elusive. This chapter aims to explore in depth some of the critical obstacles and failures that have hindered the achievement of a lasting peace in the Israeli-Palestinian conflict.

1. Historical Context

To understand the obstacles to peace, it is crucial to delve into the historical context of the conflict. The roots of the Israeli-Palestinian conflict can be traced back to the late 19th century when tensions arose due to competing nationalistic aspirations for the same land. The Zionist movement, seeking to establish a Jewish homeland in Palestine, clashed with the Arab inhabitants who felt their identity and rights were threatened. The creation of the state of Israel in 1948, followed by multiple Arab-Israeli wars, further intensified the dispute. The displacement of hundreds of thousands of Palestinians during the establishment of Israel, known as the Nakba (catastrophe), compounded the sense of deep-rooted grievances. These historical events have left scars on both sides, challenging compromise and reconciliation.

2. Political Obstacles

Numerous political obstacles have impeded progress towards a lasting peace agreement. One significant barrier is the issue of Israeli settlements in the occupied territories. Since Israel's occupation of the West Bank and East Jerusalem in 1967, Israeli governments have authorised the construction and expansion of settlements, viewed as illegal under international law. The presence of settlements has led to the confiscation of Palestinian land, the displacement of Palestinian communities, and the fragmentation of the West Bank. The expansion of settlements has created physical and psychological barriers to peace, exacerbating tensions and undermining trust between the parties involved. Additionally, the competing claims to Jerusalem, a city of profound religious and symbolic importance, have proven extremely challenging to navigate and find common ground. Each side asserts its historical and religious rights to the city, further complicating negotiations.

3. Security Concerns

The security concerns of both Israel and Palestine have played a pivotal role in obstructing efforts for sustainable peace. Israel, facing threats from militant groups and recurring attacks on its civilian population, places utmost importance on safeguarding its citizens. These security concerns have led to the establishment of a complex system of military checkpoints, the construction of physical barriers such as the separation wall, and limitations on freedom of movement for Palestinians. While these measures aim to prevent attacks and ensure the safety of Israeli citizens, they have also contributed to animosity, resentment, and a sense of collective punishment among Palestinians. The security challenges faced by the Palestinian Authority, along with internal divisions and a lack of control over the West Bank, have further complicated efforts to maintain stability and negotiate effectively.

4. Lack of Trust and Confidence

The lack of trust and confidence between the two sides has been a recurring obstacle throughout the peace process. Past failed negotiations, broken agreements, and acts of violence have deepened the mistrust, making it difficult for both parties to engage in productive dialogue. Each side perceives the other as untrustworthy and fears that compromising too much may endanger their interests and security. The absence of a shared vision for the future and a fear of compromise have hindered the development of a genuine partnership for peace. Moreover, disseminating negative narratives, lack of exposure to the other side's perspectives, and persistence of stereotypes have fuelled mutual distrust among the general population. Grassroots initiatives that foster mutual understanding and people-to-people interactions have been limited in their impact due to restrictions and political tensions.

5. Regional and International Dynamics

The Israeli-Palestinian conflict has not unfolded in isolation but has been influenced by regional and international dynamics. The engagement, or lack thereof, of neighbouring Arab states and influential global powers has considerably impacted the prospects for peace. Geopolitical rivalries, strategic interests, and competing priorities have sometimes taken precedence over pursuing a comprehensive and equitable solution. The historical support for the Palestinian cause by Arab nations, coupled with the recognition of Israel's right to exist by major powers, has played a role in shaping both the political and diplomatic landscape. However, the shifting regional dynamics, such as the recent normalisation agreements between Israel and some Arab states, have further complicated efforts to achieve a unified approach and regional consensus. The lack of a unified Arab position and the changing regional dynamics have weakened the leverage of the Palestinians in negotiations.

6. Failure of Peace Initiatives and Mediation Efforts

Numerous peace initiatives and mediation efforts have been undertaken over the years, but their failure to yield a lasting peace agreement has contributed to a sense of hopelessness and frustration. These failures have often resulted from deep-seated disagreements on core issues such as borders, refugees, and the status of Jerusalem. Additionally, the timing, sequencing, and implementation of proposed solutions have proven contentious and challenging. The Oslo Accords, for example, were hailed as a significant breakthrough in 1993, establishing the Palestinian Authority and a framework for negotiations. However, subsequent setbacks, lack of progress in final status talks, expansion of settlements, and violence have dampened hopes for a final resolution. The inability to enforce agreements, address grievances, and make meaningful progress towards a two-state solution has increased scepticism regarding future peace negotiations.

Conclusion

The obstacles and failures in achieving a lasting peace in the Israeli-Palestinian conflict are profoundly intertwined and complex. The historical, political, security-related, and psychological barriers and a lack of trust and confidence have impeded progress. The regional and international dynamics, ranging from the involvement of neighbouring Arab states to the role of global powers, have shaped and complicated the trajectory of the conflict. Despite numerous peace initiatives and mediation efforts, comprehensive resolutions have remained elusive. It is imperative that a comprehensive understanding of these obstacles and failures is developed to address them effectively and move closer to a just and sustainable resolution. The exploration of these challenges serves as a reminder of the complexities involved and underscores the need for renewed commitment, determination, and creativity in pursuing peace. Only by acknowledging these deep-rooted obstacles can genuine efforts be made to overcome them and build a future of coexistence, security, and prosperity for both Israelis and Palestinians.

CHAPTER 27

Analysis of the Impact of Failed Peace Attempts on the Conflict Dynamics

Failed peace attempts have had far-reaching consequences in the Israeli-Palestinian conflict, impacting the dynamics of the conflict itself as well as the parties involved.

This chapter delves into an in-depth analysis of the consequences and implications of these failed peace initiatives, shedding light on the reasons for their failures and their lasting effects on the current state of affairs. Understanding these impacts is crucial in identifying potential pathways towards a just and lasting peace.

UNDERSTANDING THE CONTEXT

To fully grasp the impact of failed peace attempts, it is essential to consider the historical context and the magnitude of expectations that often accompany such initiatives. Numerous peace agreements, negotiations, and frameworks have been proposed throughout the years, garnering international attention and raising hopes for a resolution. However, the protracted nature of this conflict and the complexity of the underlying issues have made the path to peace incredibly challenging.

FACTORS CONTRIBUTING TO FAILED PEACE INITIATIVES

1. Disagreements and Fundamental Differences: The Israeli-Palestinian conflict is deeply rooted in fundamental differences and entrenched narratives. Contentious issues, such as the delineation of borders, the status of Jerusalem, the right of return, and security concerns, have proven to be formidable obstacles, impeding progress in peace negotiations. These profoundly ingrained differences, shaped by historical grievances and competing national aspirations, have made it exceedingly difficult for the parties to compromise.

The delineation of borders remains a highly contentious issue with competing claims and counterclaims from both sides. Israelis argue for secure borders that protect their citizens and ensure their country's territorial integrity. On the other hand, Palestinians seek borders that reflect the pre-1967 lines, encompassing the West Bank, East Jerusalem, and the Gaza Strip. These conflicting perspectives hinder the ability to establish a mutually agreed-upon border framework.

The status of Jerusalem acts as a key sticking point, with both Israelis and Palestinians considering it their rightful capital. Overlapping religious and historical claims make any compromise on Jerusalem deeply contentious. The failure to resolve this issue further undermines trust and perpetuates the cycle of conflict.

The right of return also presents a significant obstacle, as Palestinians assert their right to return to their ancestral homes based on UN Resolution 194. Israelis, however, worry that implementing such a right would fundamentally alter their demographics and threaten the existence of the Jewish state.

Security remains a paramount concern for Israel, given its past experiences and ongoing threats. Palestinians, on the other hand, emphasise the importance of living without restrictions and military occupation. This fundamental divergence in perspectives on security has proven to be a persistent challenge in peace negotiations.

2. Lack of Trust: A long and bitter history of conflict has resulted in deep-seated mistrust between Israelis and Palestinians. This pervasive lack of trust extends to the opposing side and the peace process itself. Each party questions the other's intentions and commitment to a genuine and lasting peace. Failed attempts further erode this trust, making future negotiations more challenging and reinforcing cycles of scepticism and doubt.

Palestinians perceive Israel's continued settlement expansion in the West Bank as evidence of bad faith in negotiations. The ongoing construction of Israeli settlements deepens the sense of mistrust among Palestinians, who view it as an attempt to solidify control over disputed territories without regard for a negotiated resolution.

Similarly, Israelis feel a lack of trust due to past instances where Palestinians reneged on agreements or failed to prevent acts of violence against Israeli civilians. Terrorism, rocket attacks, and incitement to violence against Israelis have further eroded trust among Israelis, making it difficult for them to perceive Palestinians as reliable peace partners.

3. Political Calculations: Leaders on both sides of the conflict are subject to complex domestic political pressures, which can influence their stance and actions during peace negotiations. Domestic considerations, including maintaining public support, coalition politics, and concerns over undermining one's political base, can significantly impact the willingness of leaders to engage in meaningful and substantive compromises. In part, failures in the peace process can be attributed to the reluctance of political elites to make politically unpopular decisions that could endanger their hold on power.

Israeli leaders have faced challenges in balancing the aspirations of their constituents while navigating the delicate terrain of peace negotiations. The pressure to appear strong on security issues and maintain national unity often limits the flexibility of Israeli leaders in negotiating contentious issues.

On the Palestinian side, leaders face similar challenges. Divisions within Palestinian society and government structures have further complicated the peace process. The political dynamics between Fatah, which controls the Palestinian Authority, and Hamas, which governs the Gaza Strip, have hindered unified decision-making and a cohesive approach towards peace negotiations.

IMPACTS ON THE CONFLICT DYNAMICS

1. Escalation of Violence: Failed peace attempts often have dire consequences on the ground, triggering a cycle of violence and bloodshed. As disillusionment and frustration grow among the affected populations, the perception that diplomacy has failed can lead to a resurgence in violence. Radical factions and extremist elements exploit the situation, utilising it as an opportunity to further their agendas and perpetuate acts of terror. The escalation in violence not only prolongs the suffering but also deepens polarisation and reduces the prospects for future dialogue.

The failure of the Camp David Summit in 2000 resulted in a violent uprising known as the Second Intifada. The collapse of negotiations, coupled with deep-seated grievances, fuelled widespread Palestinian protests, which quickly spiralled into a wave of violence, suicide bombings, and retaliatory Israeli military actions. The cycle of violence further entrenched animosity and made renewed peace efforts more challenging.

Similarly, the breakdown of peace talks in 2014 led to the Gaza War, as Hamas initiated rocket attacks against Israeli cities while Israel responded with military incursions and airstrikes. The failure to find a political solution deepened the humanitarian crisis in Gaza, causing immense suffering for the civilian population.

2. Polarisation and Hardening of Positions: Failed peace initiatives have contributed to increased polarisation between Israeli and Palestinian societies. The breakdown of negotiations reinforces a zero-sum mindset, where each side perceives any concession as a loss. Trust diminishes, making bridging the divide and engaging constructively in future negotiations even more challenging. The hardening of positions creates an atmosphere where compromise becomes politically risky, hindering the prospects for a mutually acceptable resolution.

The lack of progress and repeated failures in the peace process have led to growing scepticism among Israelis, who increasingly question the feasibility of a negotiated settlement. This scepticism manifests in the rise of right-wing political parties advocating for a more assertive and unilateral approach to tackling security concerns.

Likewise, among Palestinians, the perceived lack of progress has fuelled frustration and disillusionment. As hopes for a two-state solution fade, alternative narratives gain traction, including calls for a single democratic state where Palestinians could achieve equal rights. These diverging views further fragment the Palestinian political landscape, making establishing a unified negotiating position challenging.

3. Weakening of Moderates: Failed peace initiatives can undermine moderate voices on both sides, sidelining those who advocate for a peaceful resolution. Frustration and disillusionment erode support for peaceful solutions, strengthening the position of hardliners who espouse more aggressive approaches. The marginalisation of moderates perpetuates the cycle of violence and further entrenches the zero-sum mentality, making it increasingly difficult for moderating influences to regain traction in the political landscape4. Regional and International Implications: Failed peace attempts in the Israeli-Palestinian conflict have broader regional and international implications, impacting relationships between Israel, Palestine, and their respective allies. The failure to achieve a peaceful resolution perpetuates regional instability and undermines efforts to address other pressing issues in the Middle East.

The Israeli-Palestinian conflict is intertwined with other regional conflicts and dynamics, making it a susceptible and interconnected issue. The inability to resolve the conflict hampers efforts to foster regional cooperation, hindered by the lingering animosity and distrust between Israelis and Palestinians.

The failure of peace attempts also strains the relationship between Israel and its Arab neighbours. Arab states, particularly those in the Gulf region, have offered peace initiatives and normalisation efforts, but these efforts depend on progress in the Israeli-Palestinian conflict. The failure to achieve a resolution undermines these regional efforts and perpetuates a sense of instability and insecurity.

The international community, including major powers and the United Nations, has invested significant diplomatic resources in the pursuit of peace in the Israeli-Palestinian conflict. The repeated failures of peace initiatives reduce international confidence in the feasibility of a negotiated settlement. This diminished confidence undermines support for future peace efforts and diminishes the international community's ability to mediate the conflict effectively.

Conclusion

Failed peace attempts have had a profound impact on the Israeli-Palestinian conflict, exacerbating violence, deepening polarisation, and hindering the prospects for a just and lasting resolution. Fundamental disagreements, lack of trust, political calculations, and regional dynamics all contribute to the difficulties in achieving peace. The consequences of failed peace initiatives extend beyond the parties directly involved, affecting regional stability and straining international relations. Recognising and understanding the impacts of these failures is imperative in developing new approaches that can address the underlying issues and move towards a sustainable solution.

CHAPTER 28

The Humanitarian Crisis

The Israeli-Palestinian conflict has had profound humanitarian consequences for the people living in Gaza and the West Bank. This chapter aims to delve deeper into the dire humanitarian crisis engulfing these territories, exploring the impact of Israeli policies, the role of international humanitarian organisations, and the conditions faced by Palestinian civilians.

1. Israeli Policies and Humanitarian Conditions

The policies and practices implemented by the Israeli government have had a significant impact on the humanitarian conditions in Gaza and the West Bank, perpetuating a cycle of suffering for the Palestinian population. Restrictive measures such as the blockade on Gaza, movement restrictions, and the construction of the separation barrier have severely limited the freedom of movement, access to essential services, and economic opportunities for Palestinians.

The blockade on Gaza, initiated in 2007, has resulted in a humanitarian disaster. It restricts the entry of essential goods, including building materials, medical supplies, and even food, leading to a severe deterioration of living conditions. The limited movement of people in and out of Gaza has also posed challenges, making access to quality healthcare and educational opportunities difficult. The deadly conflicts that have periodically erupted between Israel and Hamas have further exacerbated the dire situation, causing civilian casualties and exacerbating the trauma faced by the population.

Similarly, in the West Bank, Israeli policies such as the construction of settlements and restrictions on movement have resulted in a fragmented and isolated existence for Palestinians. The ongoing expansion of settlements, deemed illegal under international law, not only violates Palestinian rights but also severely restricts their access to land, water resources, and economic opportunities. The construction of the separation barrier, deemed illegal by the International Court of Justice, has further deepened divisions, separating families, disrupting livelihoods, and limiting access to essential services.

2. Health and Education Challenges

The Palestinian healthcare and education sectors have been greatly affected by the ongoing conflict, exacerbating the humanitarian crisis. Limited access to quality healthcare services, including medical supplies and equipment, has resulted in insufficient medical care for many Palestinians. Hospitals and clinics in Gaza, in particular, often struggle with power shortages, inadequate medical equipment, and a shortage of skilled healthcare professionals. This has led to increased mortality rates and preventable health issues. Additionally, the continued violence and psychological trauma experienced by the population have had long-lasting effects on mental health, with a significant rise in cases of post-traumatic stress disorder (PTSD) and depression.

The challenges faced by the education sector are equally alarming. Overcrowded classrooms, outdated facilities, and a lack of resources hinder the delivery of quality education. Frequent disruptions to schooling due to violence and clashes with Israeli forces have interrupted the learning process for Palestinian students, limiting their opportunities for growth and development. The Israeli military presence around schools also poses a severe threat to the safety of children and creates a hostile learning environment.

3. Water and Sanitation Crisis

Access to clean water and sanitation facilities is essential for human dignity and well-being. However, Gaza and parts of the West Bank face significant challenges. The blockade on Gaza has severely hampered the development of water and wastewater infrastructure, leading to a chronic water shortage and inadequate sanitation services. The existing infrastructure in Gaza is outdated and unable to meet the growing population's needs, risking public health and exacerbating the spread of waterborne diseases. The contamination of groundwater due to inadequate wastewater treatment poses serious health risks to the Palestinian population, including the increased incidence of water-related illnesses.

In the West Bank, Palestinians face water scarcity and restrictions on accessing their water sources. Israeli settlements consume a disproportionate amount of water, leaving inadequate supplies for Palestinians. Furthermore, the lack of access to proper sanitation facilities, particularly in vulnerable communities, severely threatens public health, further exacerbating the humanitarian crisis.

4. Food Insecurity and Dependence on Aid

The Israeli-Palestinian conflict has caused significant disruptions to agricultural activities and trade, resulting in high levels of food insecurity.

Palestinians in Gaza and parts of the West Bank face challenges in accessing nutritious and affordable food, leading to a growing dependence on international humanitarian aid. Agricultural lands, which serve as the primary source of livelihood for many Palestinians, have been destroyed due to military operations, settler violence, and access restrictions. The inability to cultivate their lands, exacerbated by the scarcity of water and adequate infrastructure, leaves many Palestinians without a means to sustain their families and results in increased poverty.

The lack of economic opportunities and high unemployment rates further contribute to food insecurity. The Israeli policies of movement restrictions, permit systems, and limitations on exports have severely impacted the Palestinian economy, preventing the development of a self-sufficient food system. As a result, Palestinians rely heavily on food aid, making them vulnerable to fluctuations in international assistance and increasing their dependence on external support.

5. The Role of International Humanitarian Organisations

International humanitarian organisations are critical in providing essential aid, services, and support to the Palestinian population affected by the conflict. These organisations work tirelessly in the face of immense challenges to alleviate the suffering and address the pressing needs of Palestinians. They collaborate with local partners and stakeholders to ensure effective and sustainable interventions, striving to promote dignity, resilience, and human rights.

However, assisting in such a complex political context is immensely challenging. Israeli restrictions and bureaucratic hurdles hinder the delivery of aid, while the frequent outbreaks of violence further complicate humanitarian operations. Israeli authorities often impose limitations on international organisations, requiring multiple permits, causing delays, and sometimes denying access altogether. Moreover, humanitarian organisations face funding constraints that limit their capacity to meet the increasing needs of the population.

Despite these challenges, international humanitarian organisations continue to work diligently, implementing health programmes, educational initiatives, water and sanitation projects, and food security interventions to improve the lives of Palestinians. They also advocate for the respect of international law and human rights and the urgency of finding a just and lasting solution to the Israeli-Palestinian conflict.

SINCE THE 7 OCTOBER 2023 ATTACK AGAINST ISRAEL

The relentless retaliation by the Israeli military has taken a toll on the lives of civilians in Gaza. Innocent men, women, and children have lost their lives or been severely injured in airstrikes and military operations. The destruction of infrastructure, housing, and essential services has further compounded the plight of Gazans. Hospitals, schools, and vital utilities have been targeted, severely limiting access to medical assistance, healthcare, and other basic needs.

Psychological and Emotional Impact

Living under the constant threat of attack has caused severe psychological trauma among Gaza's residents. The fear, stress, and uncertainty resulting from continual bombings have long-term consequences for mental health. Children, in particular, bear the brunt of this trauma, which can hinder their development and compromise their future well-being.

Economic Crisis and Displacement

The conflict has dealt a severe blow to Gaza's economy. The destruction of infrastructure, factories, and businesses has increased unemployment rates and widespread economic instability. Many residents have been displaced from their homes, becoming refugees and facing challenges in finding shelter, employment, and secure livelihoods.

Access to Basic Needs

The continual attacks have severely impacted access to basic needs in Gaza. Clean water, sanitation facilities, and electricity supply remain scarce, causing immense hardship for the population. The shortage of food, medical supplies, and other essential items has resulted in a humanitarian crisis, necessitating urgent aid and relief efforts.

Education and Future Prospects

The conflict has disrupted education in Gaza, affecting students, teachers, and educational institutions. Schools have been damaged or destroyed, making it difficult for children to continue their education. This disruption impacts their learning and hampers their prospects and opportunities for personal and professional growth.

Humanitarian Assistance and International Response

International organisations and humanitarian agencies play a crucial role in providing aid and support to the people of Gaza. However, the ongoing conflict poses challenges in delivering assistance effectively.

The international community must rally to sustain aid efforts and seek a diplomatic solution to alleviate the suffering.

The Role of Media

Media coverage and public awareness are vital in addressing the humanitarian consequences in Gaza. The media should strive for unbiased reporting, providing a comprehensive understanding of the challenges the people of Gaza face. Responsible reporting can shape public opinion and generate empathy for those affected by the conflict. Many journalists from Al-Jazeera Network paid with their lives the price of doing their job. Israel has reportedly targeted them and their families.

Potential Solutions and the Path to Peace

A lasting resolution to the Israeli-Palestinian conflict requires political will and active diplomacy. Peaceful negotiations, based on mutual respect and recognition of rights, are crucial. International involvement and cooperation are imperative for advancing peace and finding a sustainable solution.

Conclusion

The people living in Gaza face dire humanitarian consequences as a result of continual attacks from the Israeli military. The toll on civilian lives, infrastructure, and essential services is immense. Psychological trauma, economic crisis, limited access to basic needs, and disrupted education further exacerbate their plight. Urgent humanitarian assistance, sustained support, and diplomatic efforts are essential for mitigating the suffering and finding a path toward a just and lasting peace.

The dire humanitarian crisis in Gaza and the West Bank is a multifaceted issue that demands immediate attention and action. The inhumane Israeli policies, combined with the consequences of the ongoing conflict, have led to severe hardships facing the Palestinian population. Urgent steps must be taken to address the dire healthcare conditions, improve access to education, ensure clean water and sanitation facilities, and mitigate food insecurity. International cooperation, advocacy efforts, and diplomatic pressure are crucial in resolving the humanitarian crisis and restoring dignity and hope to the Palestinian people. The international community must work together to address the root causes of the conflict, dismantle barriers, and support a sustainable and inclusive solution that upholds the rights and aspirations of both Israelis and Palestinians.

CHAPTER 29

In-depth Analysis of the Humanitarian Situation in Gaza and the West Bank

The Israeli-Palestinian conflict has had far-reaching social and humanitarian consequences, particularly in the occupied territories of Gaza and the West Bank. This chapter aims to provide a comprehensive analysis of the current humanitarian situation in these areas, highlighting the challenges faced by the Palestinian population.

1. Historical Context

To fully comprehend the severity of the ongoing humanitarian crisis, it is crucial to understand the historical context in which it has developed. The Israeli occupation of the West Bank and Gaza Strip since 1967 has resulted in the displacement of thousands of Palestinians, with Israel establishing settlements in contravention of international law. The construction of separation barriers, checkpoints, and the imposition of permit systems severely restrict the movement of Palestinians, separating communities and hindering access to education, healthcare, and employment opportunities.

2. Access to Basic Necessities

The Israeli-imposed blockade on Gaza, which has been in place since 2007, has severely hampered the flow of essential goods and services into the territory. The restrictions on imports and exports have resulted in dire shortages of food, medicine, and fuel, with the World Health Organisation reporting that over half of essential medicines are at zero stock levels. Additionally, the limited availability of electricity and sanitation services further exacerbates the deteriorating living conditions, impacting the overall health and well-being of the population.

3. Healthcare System

The healthcare system in Gaza and the West Bank remains under immense strain due to long-standing structural issues compounded by the ongoing conflict. Hospitals and clinics often need adequate medical supplies, equipment, and essential medications. Due to restrictions on movement and the economic hardships faced by healthcare workers, the shortage of healthcare professionals further deteriorates the quality and accessibility of healthcare services. The dire conditions have led to increased vulnerability to disease outbreaks, particularly among children and the elderly.

4. Education and Employment

The education sector in Gaza and the West Bank faces significant challenges. Frequent closures of schools and universities due to armed conflict and insecurity disrupt the education of Palestinian children and young adults, affecting their academic development and prospects. Moreover, limited funding and resources hinder the development and maintenance of educational facilities, further compromising the quality of education. The lack of employment opportunities and high unemployment rates contribute to economic stagnation and increased dependency on external aid.

5. Displacement and Refugees

Decades of conflict and occupation have resulted in the displacement of thousands of Palestinians, leading to the creation of refugee camps and an exponential increase in the number of internally displaced persons (IDPs). The conditions in these camps often lack essential services, including reliable shelter, clean water, and adequate healthcare. The prolonged displacement exacerbates the psychological toll on affected individuals and families, impacting their overall well-being and prospects for a dignified future.

6. Human Rights Violations

Numerous reports by international organisations and human rights groups have documented widespread human rights violations perpetrated by Israeli security forces in the occupied territories. These violations include excessive use of force, arbitrary arrests and detentions, home demolitions, and restrictions on freedom of movement. The lack of accountability for these violations perpetuates a culture of impunity and undermines trust between Israeli and Palestinian communities, fuelling further tensions and escalations of violence.

7. Water Crisis

Access to clean and safe water remains a significant concern in Gaza and the West Bank. Limited access to water resources, exacerbated by Israel's control over water supplies, has led to inadequate sanitation systems, causing a rise in waterborne diseases among the Palestinian population. Moreover, the destruction of water infrastructure during conflicts and the lack of maintenance and repair exacerbate the water crisis, leading to further health risks and scarcity of this essential resource.

8. Mental Health Challenges

The prolonged conflict and living conditions have taken a heavy toll on the mental health of Palestinians in Gaza and the West Bank. The constant exposure to violence, displacement, and economic hardships contributes to high levels of stress, anxiety, depression, and PTSD among the population, especially children. Limited access to mental health services further exacerbates the situation as people struggle to cope with the psychological consequences of the conflict.

Conclusion

The humanitarian crisis in Gaza and the West Bank demands urgent attention and concerted international action. Providing immediate and sustainable assistance, ensuring the end of the blockade, and upholding human rights principles and standards are essential steps in addressing the critical conditions faced by the Palestinian population. International engagement, impartiality, and a commitment to a just resolution of the Israeli-Palestinian conflict are vital in improving the humanitarian situation and creating a path towards a more secure and prosperous future for all parties involved. The deep-rooted challenges require sustained efforts to address the immediate needs and the underlying causes of the crisis to pave the way for a long-term solution and lasting peace.

CHAPTER 30

Exploration of the Impact of Israeli Policies on Palestinian Living Conditions

In this chapter, we will explore the significant effects of Israeli policies on the living conditions of Palestinians residing in the Gaza Strip and the West Bank. By examining the various aspects of Israeli policies, we can gain a better understanding of the difficulties Palestinians face daily. It is essential to approach this discussion objectively and appreciate the complex nature of the situation. This chapter presents a detailed overview of Israeli policies' economic, social, and psychological consequences.

1. Economic Impact

Israeli policies have a significant impact on the Palestinian economy, leading to substantial socio-economic disparities between Israelis and Palestinians. One of the significant issues is the restriction of movement. Palestinians encounter numerous checkpoints, roadblocks, and the Separation Barrier, which severely impede their ability to engage in economic activities and hinder their prospects for sustainable livelihoods.

The constraints on movement not only affect an individual's ability to access job opportunities but also disrupt supply chains and hinder the growth of local industries. As a result, levels of poverty and unemployment remain high within the Palestinian population.

Moreover, the control over borders and trade imposed by Israeli policies limits Palestinian exports and imports, reducing the potential for economic growth. Palestinians face strict controls on exports, limiting their ability to expand and diversify their markets. Additionally, the reliance on Israel for imports increases the vulnerability of the Palestinian economy as it becomes subject to Israeli approval and restrictions. This dependency also leads to a trade deficit, as Palestinian imports from Israel significantly outweigh their exports, eroding the region's economic self-sufficiency.

2. Land and Resource Allocation

The allocation of land and resources plays a critical role in shaping living conditions for Palestinians. The expansion of Israeli settlements in the West Bank has resulted in the confiscation of Palestinian land, making it increasingly difficult for Palestinians to construct homes or expand their communities. The settlement enterprise encroaches upon valuable agricultural land, further suppressing Palestinian agricultural productivity and limiting food security. Moreover, the construction of the Separation Barrier has not only fragmented Palestinian land but also, in many cases, separated farmers from their fields and restricted their access to water sources critical for irrigation.

Water and agricultural resources are essential for livelihoods in an arid region like Palestine, yet Israeli policies control and restrict Palestinian access to these resources. Palestinians in the West Bank face limited access to water sources due to discriminatory water policies, resulting in significant water shortages and inadequacies in water infrastructure. Israel's control over the Mountain Aquifer, the primary water source for the region, enables them to allocate more water to Israeli settlements while limiting Palestinian access. The restrictions on water availability hinder agricultural productivity and exacerbate food insecurity, perpetuating a cycle of poverty.

3. Freedom of Movement

The severe restrictions on freedom of movement have profound effects on the daily lives of Palestinians. The imposition of checkpoints, roadblocks, and the Separation Barrier creates barriers to healthcare, education, employment, and social opportunities. Palestinians needing medical attention face extended delays, logistical challenges, and increased healthcare costs when seeking treatment, impacting their overall well-being and quality of life. Similarly, limitations on mobility hinder educational opportunities and impede Palestinians' ability to pursue higher education or attend schools outside their immediate vicinity.

In addition to physical barriers, Palestinians also face limitations on travel between the West Bank, Gaza Strip, and East Jerusalem. The densely populated Gaza Strip is subject to a strict blockade, severely restricting the movement of goods and individuals. This isolation hampers economic development, contributes to the high unemployment rate, and perpetuates a cycle of poverty and dependence on humanitarian aid. Moreover, the restriction on family visits and social connections disrupts the cultural fabric of Palestinian communities, impacting their collective identity and sense of belonging.

4. Housing and Infrastructure

Israeli policies heavily impact housing and infrastructure development in Palestinian communities. The process of obtaining building permits is complicated, expensive, and frequently subject to denial, making it nearly impossible for Palestinians to meet their housing needs legally. This leads to the growth of unlicensed Palestinian structures, which are at constant risk of demolition by Israeli authorities. Demolition orders create a constant state of insecurity and homelessness, as families may lose their homes without adequate alternatives. The demolition of homes is often justified for reasons such as lacking permits, proximity to Israeli settlements, or security concerns. This further exacerbates the already dire housing situation for Palestinians, forcing families into overcrowded living conditions or displacing them entirely.

Moreover, the lack of investment in infrastructure projects in Palestinian areas, such as road networks, electricity, water and sanitation facilities, schools, and healthcare centres, leads to inadequate access to essential services. Insufficient infrastructure hampers economic development exacerbates social inequalities and limits the overall quality of life for Palestinians. As Israel controls the entry of construction materials into the Palestinian territories, there is a significant hindrance to infrastructure projects, reinforcing the disparities between Israeli and Palestinian communities.

Conclusion

The impact of Israeli policies on Palestinian living conditions is multifaceted and far-reaching. The severe limitations placed on economic development, land and resource allocation, freedom of movement, access to essential services, and housing and infrastructure contribute to the daily challenges Palestinians face, hindering their ability to achieve a decent standard of living. Recognising and addressing these harmful policies are essential for the creation of a more equitable and sustainable future for both Israelis and Palestinians, one that upholds the principles of human rights, justice, and dignity for all.

CHAPTER 31

Examination of the Role of International Humanitarian Organisations

Amid the Israeli-Palestinian conflict, international humanitarian organisations play a crucial role in providing aid, protection, and advocacy for the civilian population living in Gaza and the West Bank. This chapter thoroughly examines these organisations' significance and impact, challenges, and role in mitigating the humanitarian crisis that has plagued the region for decades.

1. Humanitarian Organisations and their Mandate

International humanitarian organisations such as the International Committee of the Red Cross (ICRC), United Nations Relief and Works Agency for Palestine Refugees in the Near East (UNRWA), and numerous non-governmental organisations (NGOs) are guided by principles of humanitarianism, impartiality, and neutrality. Their primary objective is to alleviate human suffering, protect human rights, and provide essential services to vulnerable populations. They adhere to various frameworks, including international humanitarian law and human rights law, which serve as the foundation for their work.

2. Aid Provision and Essential Services

These organisations focus on delivering essential services vital to the survival and well-being of Palestinians living in Gaza and the West Bank. In Gaza, where the population faces severe restrictions on movement and access to essential goods, humanitarian organisations provide emergency food assistance, medical supplies, and essential hygiene kits. They also work towards rehabilitating and developing vital infrastructure, including electricity, water, and sanitation systems. In the West Bank, organisations support healthcare facilities, schools, and social welfare functions through capacity-building initiatives. Additionally, they provide psychosocial support programmes for individuals who have experienced trauma due to violence and conflict.

3. Protection of Civilians

International humanitarian organisations are critical in protecting civilians, particularly in armed conflict. They strive to ensure that civilians are not subjected to indiscriminate violence, arbitrary detention, or human rights abuses. Organisations like the ICRC monitor compliance with international humanitarian law, advocate for respecting human rights and provide legal assistance to victims. They also support efforts to prevent displacement and assist internally displaced persons. These organisations ensure that civilians can access adequate healthcare, education, and other essential services, even in the most challenging circumstances.

4. Challenges and Restrictions

Operating in a highly politicised and volatile context, international humanitarian organisations face numerous challenges in carrying out their work effectively. More funding remains a significant challenge, limiting their ability to provide adequate support to the growing number of vulnerable Palestinians. The unpredictability of the conflict, frequent escalations, and limited resources also pose challenges for these organisations. Moreover, access restrictions imposed by Israeli authorities on the movement of goods and personnel pose significant obstacles to humanitarian aid delivery. These restrictions often result in delays and increased costs and hinder the provision of timely and practical assistance. Furthermore, the ongoing division between the Palestinian factions, the political complexities surrounding the conflict, and the lack of a permanent solution contribute to the difficulties faced by these organisations.

5. Advocacy and Awareness

Beyond providing immediate assistance, international humanitarian organisations engage in advocacy efforts to raise awareness about the plight of Palestinians and push for a resolution to the Israeli-Palestinian conflict. Through public campaigns, lobbying, and engagement with governments and international bodies, they strive to ensure that the voices and rights of Palestinians are heard on the international stage. They advocate for an end to the occupation, respect for international law, and the pursuit of a just and lasting peace. By highlighting the humanitarian consequences of the conflict and sharing the stories of those affected, these organisations work to mobilise global support for the Palestinian cause and foster international solidarity.

6. Collaboration and Coordination

International humanitarian organisations recognise the importance of coordination and collaboration in maximising their impact and avoiding duplication of services. They work closely with local community organisations, government institutions, and other stakeholders to ensure a comprehensive and coordinated response in addressing the needs of Palestinians. By leveraging local knowledge and expertise, they can better understand and address the unique challenges faced by communities within the region. These organisations actively engage with local actors to ensure their interventions are contextually appropriate and sustainable.

7. The Importance of International Humanitarian Organisations

The presence and work of international humanitarian organisations are indispensable in providing immediate relief, long-term support, and protection to the Palestinian civilian population. Amidst the ongoing conflict, their presence can offer a glimmer of hope and provide a lifeline for those in distress. Through their interventions, they help preserve the dignity and rights of individuals affected by the conflict, offering a sense of normalcy in a situation of instability and uncertainty. Moreover, these organisations build community resilience, empowering individuals to overcome adversities and work towards a better future. The provision of essential services, protection, advocacy, and collaboration efforts significantly contribute to alleviating the suffering experienced by Palestinians and promoting a path towards peace.

Conclusion

International humanitarian organisations play a vital and multi-faceted role in responding to the Gaza and West Bank humanitarian crises. Despite numerous challenges, they work tirelessly to alleviate suffering, protect civilians, advocate for human rights, and promote a just resolution to the Israeli-Palestinian conflict. Their interventions offer immediate relief, support long-term development, and amplify the voices of Palestinians on a global platform. The international community must continue to support these organisations in their essential work, ensuring that the needs and rights of the Palestinian population are effectively addressed until a lasting solution is achieved. By doing so, we share a collective responsibility to alleviate the suffering and work towards a more equitable and peaceful future for all.

CHAPTER 32

The Way Forward

In light of the ongoing Israeli-Palestinian conflict, it is essential to delve deeper into potential pathways towards a just and lasting peace that can bring stability and prosperity to both Israelis and Palestinians. The complexities and challenges of the conflict may seem insurmountable, but all parties involved must continue to explore and pursue alternative solutions. This chapter will explore some possible approaches and strategies that can guide us towards a brighter future for the region.

1. Dialogue and Negotiation

Meaningful and sincere dialogue plays a pivotal role in resolving conflicts. All parties must come to the table with a genuine desire to understand each other's perspectives, acknowledge the historical grievances, and work towards finding common ground. Establishing trust and fostering an environment of open communication is crucial. Neutral mediators can provide guidance and facilitate discussions between the parties involved. This neutral presence helps create a safe space where all voices are heard and grievances can be addressed.

These negotiations must address the core issues at the heart of the conflict. These include the delineation of borders between Israel and Palestine, the status of Jerusalem, the fate of Israeli settlements in the West Bank, the right of return for Palestinian refugees, and security arrangements. All parties must engage in flexible and creative thinking to find mutually acceptable compromises that prioritise the needs and aspirations of both Israelis and Palestinians.

2. The Two-State Solution

The internationally supported two-state solution remains a widely recognised framework to address the Israeli-Palestinian conflict. This solution envisions the establishment of an independent and sovereign Palestinian state alongside a secure Israel, with defined borders based on the 1967 lines. The two-state solution addresses contentious issues such as borders, settlements, Jerusalem, and the right of return fairly and equitably.

To make the two-state solution viable, ensuring that the future Palestinian state is economically and territorially viable is crucial. This may require comprehensive land swaps, which would allow Israel to retain some significant settlement blocs while compensating the Palestinians with alternative land of equal value. Such land swaps could be negotiated based on demographic considerations and mutually agreed-upon land assessments. Jerusalem, as the holy city sacred to multiple faiths, should be the capital of Israel and Palestine, with arrangements to guarantee freedom of worship and access to all religious sites.

3. Security Cooperation

Building trust and ensuring security for both Israelis and Palestinians is paramount to any peaceful resolution. Enhanced security cooperation between Israel and the future Palestinian state can lay the foundation for stability. Joint efforts in combating terrorism, border control, intelligence sharing, and transitional justice mechanisms can foster a sense of mutual trust and cooperation.

International support and collaboration in the form of peacekeeping missions and security assistance can complement these efforts, providing a trusted presence that can help maintain security arrangements and prevent violations. Additionally, addressing the issue of illegal weapons and armed groups operating within Palestinian territories is crucial to creating a safe and stable environment for both peoples.

4. Economic Development

Economic development plays a significant role in creating a conducive environment for peace. Investing in education, infrastructure, and job creation can improve living standards and provide opportunities for Israelis and Palestinians. By enhancing economic interdependence and promoting joint economic projects, regional economic integration can contribute to more excellent stability and prosperity in the region.

International support and partnerships can facilitate economic growth on both sides of the conflict. Donor countries and organisations can provide financial aid, technical expertise, and capacity-building programmes. Implementing targeted initiatives that promote entrepreneurship, trade, tourism, and cross-border investments can create shared interests and mutual incentives for cooperation.

5. Human Rights and Justice

Recognising and addressing human rights violations and ensuring justice for both Israelis and Palestinians is essential for long-term peace. Establishing truth and reconciliation commissions, empowering judicial systems, and promoting accountability can contribute to healing and building trust between the parties.

Transitional justice mechanisms, such as truth commissions or special tribunals, can provide a platform for victims of violence and human rights abuses to share their experiences and seek redress. Acknowledging past injustices, compensating victims, and holding those responsible accountable can pave a path to forgiveness and reconciliation. This process can address grievances, foster social healing, and lay the foundation for a just society and sustainable peace.

6. International Support and Engagement

The international community is vital in supporting and facilitating the peace process. Regional and international actors should continue to engage in diplomatic efforts, providing political, economic, and security assistance to the parties involved. When judiciously applied, international pressure, incentives, and sanctions can help steer the parties towards constructive dialogue and compromise.

The principles of international law, including United Nations resolutions and the Fourth Geneva Convention, should serve as guiding principles for any negotiated settlement. The International Criminal Court may also play a role in holding accountable individuals who have committed war crimes or violated human rights during the conflict.

It is crucial to ensure that any solution is comprehensive, fair, and takes into account the aspirations and rights of both Israelis and Palestinians. Peace-making will require immense political will, compromise, and resilience from all parties involved.

In conclusion, the way forward demands a commitment to dialogue, a focus on shared aspirations, and a genuine willingness to address concerns and grievances. Pursuing peace must prioritise the dignity, security, and rights of all individuals affected by the conflict. By embracing inclusive and constructive approaches, we can pave the way towards a future where Israelis and Palestinians coexist in peace, prosperity, and harmony. The time to act is now; the path to peace begins with our collective dedication to this worthy cause.

CHAPTER 33

Assessment of Potential Pathways Towards a Just and Lasting Peace

This chapter will explore potential pathways towards a just and lasting peace between Israel and Palestine. It is crucial to approach this subject with a professional and objective lens to assess viable options to address the underlying issues and establish a sustainable solution for both parties involved. While it is essential to acknowledge the complexities and challenges inherent in the Israeli-Palestinian conflict, it is equally important to remain hopeful and open to new ideas. Let us delve into potential pathways that can pave the way for a peaceful resolution.

1. Diplomatic Negotiations

Diplomatic negotiations between Israel and Palestine have been ongoing for decades. Revising these negotiations with sincere commitment from both sides and the international community is crucial. Dialogue should address core issues such as borders, security, settlements, refugees, and the status of Jerusalem. Both parties must be willing to make compromises and engage in substantive discussions guided by international law and fairness principles.

Efforts must be made to establish a framework that addresses the aspirations and concerns of both Israelis and Palestinians. This can be achieved by exploring creative solutions, such as land swaps, that ensure the viability of a future Palestinian state while addressing security considerations for Israel. Additionally, a just resolution for Palestinian refugees should be pursued, taking into account their right of return or appropriate compensation. As a profoundly significant city for both sides, Jerusalem's status necessitates a balanced and shared approach that respects religious, historical, and cultural sensitivities.

2. International Mediation

Utilising internationally recognised mediators, such as the United Nations or prominent nations with impartiality and credibility, can help bridge the divide between Israel and Palestine. A neutral mediator can provide a platform for structured negotiations, ensuring a fair and balanced process. Encouraging the active participation of these mediators, reinforcing trust-building mechanisms, and promoting confidence-building measures can create an environment conducive to peace talks.

International mediators should be equipped with the necessary resources and support to facilitate discussions, manage disputes, and mediate between the parties. They should be empowered to propose creative solutions and assist in implementing agreed-upon measures. A comprehensive peace plan that includes viable security arrangements, economic cooperation, and mechanisms for dispute resolution can serve as a roadmap for a just and lasting settlement.

3. Peacebuilding Initiatives

Peacebuilding initiatives play a crucial role in establishing trust, fostering dialogue, and cultivating understanding between the Israeli and Palestinian communities. Civil society organisations, religious leaders, and grassroots movements should be encouraged and supported to foster cooperation, tolerance, and reconciliation at the societal level. Initiatives that promote cultural exchange programmes, economic cooperation, and joint infrastructure projects can lay the foundation for future peaceful coexistence.

Education plays a vital role in building a lasting peace. Educational curricula on both sides need to promote understanding, respect, and empathy for the other's narrative and rights. Encouraging joint educational programmes and platforms that promote dialogue and critical thinking can shape a new generation that values peaceful coexistence.

4. Humanitarian Interventions

Addressing the dire humanitarian situation in Gaza and the West Bank is of paramount importance in the pursuit of peace. Providing immediate relief and assistance to alleviate suffering should be prioritised, ensuring access to necessities such as food, water, healthcare, and education. Furthermore, efforts should improve socio-economic conditions and empower local communities, offering them a sense of dignity and hope for a better future.

Investments in sustainable development projects, infrastructure, and job creation can contribute to long-term stability and prosperity. Economic cooperation and integration, where Palestinians can access their resources and develop a viable economy, are crucial for creating conditions that reduce tension and provide an incentive for peace.

5. International Law and Accountability

Adherence to international law and ensuring accountability for violations is essential in any peace process. International bodies and organisations should work collectively to monitor and address human rights abuses, settlement expansion, and other actions undermining the prospects for peace. A commitment to justice and fairness will foster trust and confidence between the parties, making a lasting peace possible.

The international community should pressure both parties to halt any actions that contravene international law or cause harm to civilians. This includes illegal settlement construction, house demolitions, indiscriminate attacks, and targeted killings. Upholding the rule of law and promoting respect for human rights creates an environment conducive to trust and peaceful coexistence.

6. Regional Engagement

Engaging regional powers, neighbouring countries, and Arab states in the peace process can provide valuable support and stability. Collaborative efforts to address shared interests, such as security concerns and economic development, can create an enabling environment for progress. Regional support can also ensure that any agreed-upon peace agreement is upheld and implemented effectively.

Regional powers can significantly support economic investments, joint ventures, and cross-border initiatives that foster cooperation and integration. Arab states can provide political, economic, and diplomatic backing, leveraging their influence to encourage the recognition of

Israel and to ensure the implementation of peace agreements. Regional cooperation and integration can help build bridges and promote a sense of shared destiny among peoples in the region.

Conclusion

Achieving a just and lasting peace between Israel and Palestine requires a genuine commitment from both parties, supported by the international community. It demands a comprehensive approach that addresses the concerns of Palestinians and Israelis alike, focusing on the core issues while promoting understanding, respect, and trust. By pursuing diplomatic negotiations, involving impartial mediators, engaging in peacebuilding initiatives, addressing humanitarian needs, upholding international law, and seeking regional engagement, we can pave the way for a future where Israelis and Palestinians coexist in peace, security, and prosperity. Through these pathways, we can sow the seeds of a brighter and harmonious future for all.

CHAPTER 34

Exploration of Alternative Solutions to the Israeli-Palestinian Conflict

In this chapter, we will explore different alternative solutions to the Israeli-Palestinian conflict. The conflict has been ongoing for a long time, and it is important to examine all potential options that could bring about a fair and lasting resolution. We will provide a detailed overview of these solutions, taking into account their feasibility, practicality, and ability to maintain peace in the region.

1. Two-State Solution

The two-state solution has remained the primary approach for resolving the Israeli-Palestinian conflict. This proposal suggests the establishment of an independent Palestinian state alongside Israel, with defined borders and self-governance. Negotiations would address sensitive issues such as the status of Jerusalem, the return of Palestinian refugees, and the Israeli settlements in the West Bank.

One key obstacle to the two-state solution is the geographical fragmentation caused by Israeli settlements. As these settlements continue to expand, the feasibility of creating a contiguous and viable Palestinian state becomes increasingly challenging. Additionally, security concerns for both Israelis and Palestinians play a vital role in negotiations. The question of borders, access to resources, freedom of movement, and the demilitarization of a future Palestinian state is crucial to guaranteeing security for both sides.

Another contentious issue revolves around the status of Jerusalem, with both Israelis and Palestinians regarding it as their capital. A fundamental challenge is finding a mutually acceptable solution that respects Jerusalem's religious, historical, and cultural significance.

Furthermore, addressing the right of return for Palestinian refugees is a susceptible matter. Palestinians argue for their right to return to their ancestral lands, while Israelis fear that large-scale return would threaten their demographic majority.

Renewed efforts are necessary to rebuild trust, engage in direct negotiations, and address the economic and humanitarian disparity between the two parties. The international community and regional actors must also actively support and facilitate the two-state solution.

2. One-State Solution

The one-state solution is an alternative proposition that suggests the creation of a single democratic state encompassing the current territory of Israel, the West Bank, and Gaza, in which Israelis and Palestinians would have equal rights and opportunities. Advocates argue that this approach would surpass the current system of segregation and offer a more inclusive and equitable society.

Implementing a one-state solution faces significant challenges. Reconciling competing national identities is a crucial concern. Israelis and Palestinians have different historical narratives, understandings of their relationship with the land, and cultural attachments to specific regions. Overcoming these differences and fostering a shared national identity that respects and acknowledges the narratives of both parties would be a monumental undertaking.

Addressing historical grievances is another significant challenge. The conflict's intricate history features numerous instances of violence, displacement, and loss on both sides. Acknowledging and reconciling these past injustices while ensuring justice and healing is a complex, emotional, and delicate endeavour.

Ensuring equal representation and protecting minority rights within a unified state is vital for an equitable society. Although a one-state solution theoretically promises equal rights for all, the practicality of achieving this in a deeply divided society requires profound institutional overhaul, inclusive governance structures, and mechanisms to safeguard minority rights.

Preserving both the Jewish and Palestinian Arab character of the state is another significant consideration. Balancing national and cultural aspirations while respecting each group's demographic realities and historical attachments requires a delicate political balance.

Transitioning from a reality of prolonged conflict and segregation to a shared state requires exceptional goodwill, compromise, and extensive political, legal, and administrative restructuring. The numerous challenges associated with the one-state solution make it a more radical departure from the current status quo, thus requiring comprehensive planning, consultations, and consensus from the parties involved.

3. Confederation Model

The confederation model proposes a cooperative framework where Israel, Palestine, and potentially neighbouring countries would form a confederation. This model envisions shared decision-making, security cooperation, and economic integration to address common challenges and facilitate coexistence.

The confederation model acknowledges the interconnected nature of the conflict and seeks regional solutions. It recognizes the interdependencies between Israelis and Palestinians, encompassing political and security dimensions and economic, environmental, and social aspects.

Successful implementation would require extensive negotiations to redefine territorial boundaries, security arrangements, and the distribution of resources. Overcoming historical animosities and political differences between Israel and Palestine, as well as engaging neighbouring countries, would be essential to ensure the stability and sustainability of a confederation.

The confederation model highlights the importance of collaboration and regional cooperation in addressing the Israeli-Palestinian conflict. By fostering shared interests, mutual accountability, and addressing common challenges such as water scarcity, energy resources, and economic development, a confederation could create a framework for enhanced cooperation and coexistence.

4. *International Trusteeship*

Under the auspices of the United Nations or other regional actors, an international trusteeship offers an alternative approach to addressing the Israeli-Palestinian conflict. This solution suggests an interim period where a neutral international body assumes responsibility for governing the disputed territories, overseeing their development, and ensuring the protection of the rights and security of both Israelis and Palestinians.

The goals of an international trusteeship would be to build trust, establish stability, and lay the groundwork for future negotiations. By temporarily taking the governance of the region out of the hands of the conflicting parties, an international trusteeship can provide a neutral space for rebuilding trust and confidence between Israelis and Palestinians.

The success of an international trusteeship depends on securing the trust and cooperation of all parties involved. Additionally, a robust monitoring and enforcement mechanism, as well as clear guidelines for the eventual transfer of governance to Israelis and Palestinians, would need to be established.

International trusteeship could provide an opportunity for the international community to engage in the resolution process actively, ensuring impartiality and reducing the burdens on both Israel and Palestine. However, it would also require overcoming potential political obstacles and fostering the commitment of all parties involved.

5. *Grassroots and Civil Society Initiatives*

Grassroots movements and civil society initiatives are vital in fostering dialogue and trust-building between Israelis and Palestinians. These initiatives encourage people-to-people interactions, joint projects, cultural exchange, and mutual understanding.

Supporting and expanding grassroots and civil society initiatives can create an atmosphere conducive to peace by promoting mutual understanding, deconstructing stereotypes, and humanizing the "other. Such initiatives involve educational programs, dialogue forums, youth exchanges, economic cooperation, and joint health, technology, and arts initiatives.

By engaging individuals at the grassroots level, these initiatives contribute to building peace from the ground up, fostering relationships, and generating a sense of shared humanity. They also push for societal change, challenging existing narratives and promoting empathy and tolerance.

Efforts to support grassroots initiatives should focus on facilitating access to funding, resources, and capacity-building opportunities. Governments, international organizations, and civil society actors can play a significant role in supporting and amplifying the work of grassroots peacebuilders, providing platforms for collaboration and scaling up their impact.

Conclusion

The Israeli-Palestinian conflict's entrenched complexities demand a thorough exploration of alternative solutions. We broaden our understanding of potential paths towards a peaceful resolution by considering proposals such as the two-state solution, one-state solution, confederation model, international trusteeship, and grassroots initiatives. These alternative solutions present distinct challenges and practicalities arising from political, historical, cultural, and emotional factors.

Ultimately, the path to a just and lasting resolution lies in a combination of political will, genuine dialogue, compromise, and addressing the root causes of the conflict. The international community and regional actors must continue to actively support and facilitate negotiations, provide resources and expertise, and hold all parties accountable for their commitments.

While the two-state solution has long been the focus of negotiations, its feasibility and viability are increasingly questioned due to ongoing settlement expansion and political challenges. However, it remains a widely supported solution and one that offers the potential for both Israelis and Palestinians to have their states living side by side in peace and security. Any proposed alternative solution must carefully consider the implications for both parties, taking into account historical and cultural attachments, security concerns, and the aspirations and rights of both Israelis and Palestinians.

The one-state solution, confederation model, and international trusteeship offer alternative approaches that aim to address the inherent complexities of the conflict. These proposals raise important questions about national identities, minority rights, shared governance, and regional cooperation. Implementing any of these solutions would require a comprehensive and inclusive process that acknowledges all parties' grievances, aspirations, and fears.

Grassroots and civil society initiatives foster dialogue, empathy, and understanding between Israelis and Palestinians. While they may not provide a comprehensive solution to the conflict, these initiatives contribute to building a foundation of trust and cooperation, challenging existing narratives, and nurturing relationships that can help pave the way for future negotiations and peacebuilding efforts.

In conclusion, the exploration of alternative solutions to the Israeli-Palestinian conflict is necessary to broaden our understanding and move towards a just and lasting resolution. The two-state solution, one-state solution, confederation model, international trusteeship, and grassroots initiatives each offer unique perspectives and challenges. By engaging in genuine dialogue, addressing historical grievances, promoting trust-building measures, and involving the international community and regional actors, there is hope for a future where Israelis and Palestinians can coexist in peace, security, and mutual respect.

CHAPTER 35

Discussion on the Importance of International Pressure and Engagement

In the pursuit of a just and lasting resolution to the Israeli-Palestinian conflict, the role of international pressure and engagement cannot be overstated. This chapter delves into the significance of international involvement in pushing for a fair and equitable outcome. By examining the historical context, international actors, potential strategies, challenges faced, and the potential impact, we can comprehend the complex dynamics of international pressure and engagement in the conflict.

The Historical Context

Recognising the historical precedents that have shaped the Israeli-Palestinian conflict is crucial to understanding the importance of international pressure and engagement.

The conflict traces its roots to the late 19th century with the emergence of the Zionist movement. This movement aimed to establish a Jewish homeland in Palestine. This movement gained traction amidst rising anti-Semitism in Europe and the growing desire for self-determination among Jewish communities. However, the establishment of the State of Israel in 1948 led to the displacement and dispossession of Palestinians. This event, known as the Nakba or "catastrophe," provoked deep-seated grievances and resistance among Palestinians.

Over the years, numerous attempts at peace, including the Oslo Accords in the 1990s, have faltered, highlighting the need for external intervention. International pressure has often been essential in bridging gaps, fostering dialogue, and encouraging meaningful negotiations between the parties involved. It is important to note that while both Israelis and Palestinians have legitimate claims and aspirations, the power dynamics between the two sides are asymmetric, with Israel benefiting from a more robust military and political position. International pressure has helped balance these asymmetries and push for a just and equitable resolution to the conflict.

International Actors

The international community comprises various actors, each with the potential to contribute to promoting peace and resolving the conflict. Governments, intergovernmental organisations, non-governmental organisations, and influential individuals all play a role in exerting pressure and engaging in the Israeli-Palestinian conflict.

Governments, particularly those with influence and leverage, are pivotal in exerting pressure on the involved parties and facilitating dialogue. The United States has traditionally been a critical player in the Israeli-Palestinian conflict, both due to its strategic alliance with Israel and its attempts to broker peace agreements. However, domestic factors and other geopolitical considerations have often hindered its influence.

The European Union has been actively participating by providing financial aid and diplomatic support and promoting a two-state solution. European countries have played a significant role in funding development projects, promoting economic cooperation, and providing humanitarian aid to the Palestinian territories.

Regional organisations, such as the Arab League, have played a critical role in supporting the Palestinian cause and promoting Arab-Israeli dialogue. Their involvement has helped provide a united Arab front in negotiations and generated momentum for peace initiatives. Through its various agencies, the United Nations has been instrumental in addressing issues such as refugees, human rights, and international law in the context of the Israeli-Palestinian conflict. The United Nations Relief and Works Agency for Palestine Refugees in the Near East (UNRWA) has provided vital services to Palestinian refugees since its establishment in 1949.

Additionally, non-governmental organisations (NGOs), through their grassroots activities and public awareness campaigns, have the power to mobilise public opinion and foster dialogue at the societal level. These organisations often work on the ground, providing humanitarian assistance, monitoring human rights violations, and advocating for the rights of both Israelis and Palestinians. They play a crucial role in documenting and exposing violations of international law, increasing public awareness, and pressuring governments to take action.

Strategies for International Pressure and Engagement:
Various strategies can be employed to apply international pressure and engagement effectively. Economic sanctions, diplomatic measures, and political leverage are tools that international actors can utilise to influence the behaviour and policies of the parties involved.

Economic pressure can involve cutting off financial aid or imposing trade restrictions on parties non-compliant with peace negotiations.

Boycott, Divestment, and Sanctions (BDS) campaigns have gained traction in recent years, urging individuals, organisations, and governments to refrain from engaging with Israeli institutions and companies involved in the occupation of Palestinian territories. While controversial, proponents argue that BDS can serve as a nonviolent means to pressure Israel to change its policies.

Diplomatic initiatives, such as peace summits, negotiations, and mediation efforts, have the potential to bring parties together to explore mutually agreeable solutions. The Quartet on the Middle East, which comprises the United Nations, the United States, the European Union, and Russia, has been at the forefront of international mediation efforts. With varying degrees of success, international actors have attempted to broker peace agreements and create frameworks for negotiations to establish a viable and independent Palestinian state alongside Israel.

Legal mechanisms also play a role in pressuring parties to adhere to international law and seek accountability for human rights violations. International court proceedings offer a platform for addressing grievances and ensuring justice. The International Criminal Court (ICC) has the authority to investigate and prosecute individuals responsible for serious crimes committed in the Israeli-Palestinian context, although its jurisdiction remains a subject of contention.

International actors must coordinate and collaborate, as collective pressure yields a more significant impact than fragmented efforts. By aligning their actions and messages, governments, intergovernmental organisations, and NGOs can communicate that the conflict requires urgent resolution based on human rights principles, international law, and the right to self-determination.

Challenges

While international pressure and engagement are critical, the Israeli-Palestinian conflict presents several challenges that impede progress. Firstly, geopolitical interests and power dynamics influence the positions of international actors. The influence of the United States, for instance, on the peace process has often been influenced by its strategic ties with Israel. Similarly, other countries may prioritise their political or economic interests when engaging in the conflict, challenging adequate pressure.

Secondly, extremism and violence on both sides erode trust and derail peace efforts. The rise of militant groups, such as Hamas, has posed significant obstacles to negotiations. Acts of terrorism, rocket attacks, and retaliatory measures perpetuate a cycle of violence and create an environment of fear and hostility. The challenge of disarming these groups and fostering a climate of nonviolence is an integral part of achieving a just and lasting resolution.

Moreover, historical grievances, deeply rooted nationalism, and cultural nuances complicate the conflict and make it challenging to find common ground. The narratives and historical narratives of Israelis and Palestinians often clash, exacerbating distrust and hampering reconciliation efforts. Addressing these narratives and understanding both parties' underlying motivations and aspirations will be vital in fostering a more constructive dialogue.

Lastly, the shifting political landscape in the region and global arena underscores the need for adaptive and flexible strategies. Conflict dynamics in the broader Middle East, such as the Arab uprisings, the rise of non-state actors, and regional power struggles, can either facilitate or hinder progress towards a resolution. The changing dynamics between major international players, such as the United States, Russia, and major

European powers, can also impact their positions and involvement in the conflict.

The Potential Impact

Increased international pressure and engagement can have significant ramifications for the Israeli-Palestinian conflict. A unified international stance rooted in principles of justice, equality, and respect for human rights can empower moderate voices on both sides, helping them navigate the complexities of the conflict and push for a just and lasting resolution.

International pressure and engagement can help level the playing field between Israel and Palestine, addressing the power asymmetries that exist between the two parties. By advocating for adherence to international law, human rights, and the principles of self-determination, international actors can hold both sides accountable for their actions and create an environment conducive to negotiations.

Transparency and accountability are crucial in the Israeli-Palestinian conflict. International pressure can help ensure that human rights violations, international law, and humanitarian principles are documented, condemned, and addressed. This includes holding accountable those who commit war crimes, acts of terror, and systematic human rights abuses. Such actions can deter future violations and contribute to a culture of respect for human rights.

International pressure and engagement can also help address the core issues fueling the conflict, such as the status of Jerusalem, borders, settlements, and the right of return for Palestinian refugees. By facilitating negotiations and offering frameworks for resolution, international actors can help bridge the gaps between the parties and find mutually acceptable solutions to these contentious issues.

Moreover, international pressure and engagement can foster trust-building and confidence-building measures between Israelis and Palestinians. People-to-people exchanges, cultural initiatives, and educational programs can help humanise the "other," dispel stereotypes and promote understanding and empathy. These initiatives can significantly contribute to creating an environment where meaningful dialogue and reconciliation can take place.

Furthermore, international pressure and engagement can provide the Palestinian territories with economic support and development opportunities. By investing in infrastructure, education, healthcare, and job creation, international actors can help alleviate Palestinians' socio-economic challenges, providing them with the necessary foundation for a viable and independent state. Economic cooperation between Israelis and Palestinians can also contribute to building bridges and promoting cooperation beyond the conflict.

Conclusion

The Israeli-Palestinian conflict is a complex and profoundly entrenched issue, with longstanding grievances on both sides. International pressure and engagement are crucial in addressing the power imbalances, fostering dialogue, and pushing for a peaceful resolution. By leveraging economic, diplomatic, and legal mechanisms, international actors can exert meaningful pressure and hold parties accountable. However, they must also navigate geopolitical interests, extremism, historical grievances, and shifting regional dynamics. With a united and cohesive international approach, there is a more significant potential to pave the way for a peaceful future based on principles of justice, equality, and respect for human rights.

CHAPTER 36

Conclusion

In this book, we have embarked on an extensive and profound journey to understand the complexities and nuances of the Israeli-Palestinian conflict. Our exploration has delved deep into the historical, religious, political, and humanitarian dimensions that have shaped this enduring dispute. Throughout the preceding pages, it has become increasingly clear that the conflict cannot be reduced to a simplistic narrative of winners and losers or a quest for dominance; instead, it is a deeply rooted struggle for land, identity, self-determination, and security for both Israelis and Palestinians.

The Israeli-Palestinian conflict traces its origins back to centuries of history, marked by conflicting claims to the land and intertwined with religious convictions. The aspirations and motivations of both Israelis and Palestinians have been shaped by this historical backdrop, fuelling their determination to achieve their respective goals. Over time, the narrative of the conflict has shifted and transformed, influenced by international events, changing regional dynamics, and evolving perceptions of national and collective identity. Understanding the historical context is crucial in comprehending the deep-seated roots of the conflict.

Furthermore, this conflict is intricately entwined with political considerations and power dynamics. Israel's military superiority, advanced weaponry, and well-structured defence forces have often granted it a position of relative dominance. However, it is essential to recognise that military might alone cannot secure a lasting victory or guarantee peace. The complexities of the conflict require a comprehensive approach that addresses the underlying causes and aspirations of both Israelis and Palestinians, encompassing political, economic, social, and security dimensions. It is through a holistic approach that a sustainable solution can be reached, one that ensures the security and well-being of both parties.

The international community has played a significant role in the Israeli-Palestinian conflict, attempting to facilitate a peaceful resolution and mitigate the escalation of violence. Numerous peace initiatives, negotiations, and diplomatic efforts have been pursued, driven by a collective desire for peaceful regional peace. However, the complexities of the conflict, coupled with entrenched positions, diverging interests, and geopolitical dynamics, have hindered progress towards a resolution.

Throughout this book, we have also explored the impact of psychological warfare, propaganda, and the weaponisation of information. The narrative surrounding the Israeli-Palestinian conflict is highly contested, with each side employing various communication strategies to shape public perception and secure international support. Understanding how narratives are constructed, disseminated, and received is crucial in comprehending the multiple layers of the conflict and the challenges it poses for reaching a shared understanding.

Moreover, the profound humanitarian crisis that has unfolded in Gaza and the West Bank cannot be ignored. Palestinians have endured dire living conditions exacerbated by restrictions on movement, limited access to essential resources, and ongoing violence. Humanitarian organisations have tirelessly provided much-needed relief, yet the underlying causes of the crisis persist. Addressing the humanitarian dimensions of the conflict is essential, not only for the well-being of Palestinians but also for fostering an environment conducive to dialogue and lasting peace.

The influence and engagement of Arab governments in the region have also shaped events and influenced the trajectory of the conflict. Political calculations, regional stability concerns, and solidarity with the Palestinian cause have all shaped Arab governments' positions. Despite their historical support for Palestinians, navigating the complexities of regional dynamics and maintaining strategic alliances has, at times, constrained their impact on the conflict. Balancing diverse interests and maintaining stability within their borders have often been significant considerations.

Furthermore, the global Muslim response to the Israeli-Palestinian conflict has been resolute. Muslim communities worldwide have consistently expressed solidarity and support for the Palestinian cause, driven by shared historical, cultural, and religious ties. This global support carries significant weight and can influence regional dynamics and shape perceptions of Muslims globally. The impact of this support extends beyond political calculations and has the potential to shape the discourse surrounding the conflict on a global scale.

As we conclude this profound exploration, it becomes evident that the Israeli-Palestinian conflict defies simplistic dichotomies and calls for a comprehensive, multidimensional solution. Achieving a peaceful peace requires sustained international pressure, collective engagement from all relevant stakeholders, and an unwavering commitment to dialogue. Genuine dialogue, grounded in mutual respect, recognition, and understanding, is essential for transcending the deeply entrenched narratives, fostering trust, and finding common ground.

Going forward, addressing the Israeli-Palestinian conflict requires an unwavering commitment to upholding human rights, dignity, and equality for all parties involved. It necessitates a focus on structural and systemic issues, addressing the fundamental causes of the conflict and ensuring that all individuals have the opportunity to prosper. Balancing the aspirations and rights of Israelis and Palestinians requires creative and courageous leadership that transcends the limitations of previous negotiations and seeks innovative solutions.

In closing, let us remember that the Israeli-Palestinian conflict transcends simplistic notions of victory and defeat. It calls for genuine recognition of all involved's shared humanity, rights, and aspirations. A sustainable and equitable peace can be achieved only through a sincere dedication to dialogue, a commitment to justice, and the upholding of human rights. The path ahead may be challenging, but our collective responsibility is to strive for a future where dignity, coexistence, and peace prevail, leaving a legacy of reconciliation and understanding for future generations.

CHAPTER 37

Recapitulation of Key Arguments Presented Throughout the Book

Throughout this book, we have explored the intricacies of the Israeli-Palestinian conflict, delving into its historical roots, complex dynamics, and potential paths towards resolution. In this final chapter, we will comprehensively recapitulate the critical arguments presented throughout the book to understand the conflict and its possible solution better.

1. The Historical Context

To fully comprehend the Israeli-Palestinian conflict, understanding its historical context is crucial. The conflict emerged against the backdrop of the Zionist movement's aspirations for a Jewish homeland and the subsequent Arab resistance to Jewish immigration and land acquisition. The Balfour Declaration of 1917 and the League of Nations' endorsement of the British Mandate in Palestine further compounded the tensions. The 1947 United Nations Partition Plan and the subsequent

1948 Arab-Israeli war resulted in the displacement and dispossession of Palestinians on a significant scale, leading to the formation of the State of Israel and the Palestinian refugee crisis. The occupation of the West Bank, East Jerusalem, and Gaza Strip during the 1967 Six-Day War further complicated the conflict's dynamics.

2. The Palestinian Perspective

For Palestinians, the conflict represents an ongoing struggle for self-determination and statehood. Deep attachments to their ancestral lands, coupled with the aspirations for freedom, justice, and the right of return for refugees, fuel their resistance against Israeli policies. Palestinians' national identity is deeply intertwined with their cultural heritage, religious sites, and the collective memory of dispossession and displacement. Acknowledging and addressing these grievances is crucial for any sustainable resolution.

3. Israeli Military Dominance

Israel's military capabilities and technological advancements have granted it a significant advantage in the conflict. By establishing a robust defence infrastructure, Israel has been able to protect its citizens during periods of conflict. However, it is imperative to recognise that solely relying on military might does not guarantee long-term peace. Addressing the root causes of the conflict, such as land disputes, settlement expansion, and the question of Palestinian statehood, is necessary for a sustainable resolution.

4. The Role of the International Community

The international community has played a prominent role throughout the conflict through diplomatic efforts and financial aid. Various states and organisations have aligned themselves with either the Israelis or Palestinians, often driven by their national interests or historical connections. The international community's lack of a unified and impartial approach has hindered progress, emphasising the need for a more concerted effort to broker a just and lasting resolution. The international community should utilise the United Nations and other multilateral platforms to promote dialogue, encourage compromise, and hold both parties accountable for their actions.

5. Psychological Warfare and Propaganda

Psychological warfare and the manipulation of narratives have become intrinsic aspects of the Israeli-Palestinian conflict. Both sides employ tactics to shape public perceptions, challenging the truth and perpetuating biases. Media coverage, social media, and public discourse are often battlegrounds for competing narratives, further polarising perspectives. Encouraging critical analysis of information, promoting fact-based reporting, and fostering open dialogues are crucial steps towards overcoming these manipulations.

6. The Role of Arab Governments

Arab governments hold significant influence in the Israeli-Palestinian conflict. While some Arab nations have prioritised the Palestinian cause, extending political, financial, and humanitarian support, regional geopolitical dynamics and divergent political approaches have complicated comprehensive efforts. The unity and collective effort of Arab governments in advocating for Palestinian rights will be vital for achieving a just and lasting resolution. Arab governments should work together to strengthen diplomatic ties and provide sustainable support to Palestinians, both politically and economically.

7. *The Global Muslim Response*

Muslims worldwide have consistently shown solidarity with the Palestinians, driven by religious, ethical, and humanitarian considerations. From political support to financial contributions and grassroots activism, the global Muslim response has played an essential role in highlighting the plight of Palestinians and pressuring governments to take a firm stance. Leveraging this support to encourage positive engagement and peaceful dialogue is critical for resolving the conflict. Engaging with religious leaders, civil society organisations, and influential Muslim figures can foster understanding and contribute to efforts towards a just and lasting peace.

8. *Attempts at Peace and Their Failures*

Peace negotiations and initiatives have succeeded or faltered throughout the conflict's history. Key milestones include the Oslo Accords, the Camp David Summit, the Annapolis Conference, and, more recently, the failed attempts at the United States-led peace plan known as the "Deal of the Century." Unresolved issues, including borders, settlements, the right of return, security arrangements, and Jerusalem's status, have repeatedly hindered the parties' ability to reach a mutually agreed-upon resolution. Recognising the failures and learning from past mistakes is essential in paving the way for future negotiations.

9. The Humanitarian Crisis

The prolonged Israeli occupation and the blockade of Gaza have resulted in a severe humanitarian crisis in the Palestinian territories. Palestinians in the West Bank and Gaza endure restrictions on movement, limited access to essential resources, demolitions, forced displacement, and a lack of economic opportunities. The international humanitarian community, including organisations like the United Nations Relief and Works Agency for Palestine Refugees (UNRWA), plays a vital role in providing essential services and addressing the urgent needs of Palestinians affected by the conflict. International support should be sustained and expanded to alleviate the suffering and promote socio-economic development.

10. The Way Forward

Achieving a just and lasting peace requires recognising the multifaceted nature of the Israeli-Palestinian conflict and acknowledging the rights and aspirations of both Israelis and Palestinians. A comprehensive approach encompassing political negotiations, social reconciliation, economic development, and cultural understanding is necessary. International pressure, diplomatic engagement, grassroots efforts, and civil society initiatives are all essential in fostering a conducive environment for negotiations and building trust between the parties. Addressing key issues such as borders, settlements, the right of return, security arrangements, and Jerusalem's status will require compromise and a genuine commitment from all parties involved.

Conclusion

In conclusion, the Israeli-Palestinian conflict is deeply rooted in history, political complexities, and unresolved grievances. By understanding and addressing these intricacies, acknowledging the legitimate aspirations and rights of both Israelis and Palestinians and working towards a more impartial international approach, we can lay the groundwork for a just and lasting resolution. Our collective responsibility is to seize this opportunity and work towards a future where both nations can coexist in peace, security, and prosperity.

CHAPTER 38

Call to Action For a Fair Resolution to the Israeli-Palestinian Conflict

The Israeli-Palestinian conflict has persisted for far too long, causing immense suffering for both sides. It is imperative that we now come together as a global community and collectively strive towards a fair resolution that respects the rights, aspirations, and dignity of both Israelis and Palestinians. A fundamental shift in approach and mindset is required to break the cycle of violence and bring about lasting peace in the region.

Historical Context and Narrative Acknowledgement

Understanding the historical context of the Israeli-Palestinian conflict is crucial for charting a path towards a fair resolution. In the late 19th century, the Zionist movement emerged in Europe to establish a Jewish homeland in Palestine, driven by the desire to create a haven for Jewish people in the wake of widespread anti-Semitism and persecution.

However, the establishment of a Jewish homeland in a land already inhabited by a majority Arab Palestinian population led to a collision of aspirations and claims to the same territory. This clash of narratives has fuelled the conflict for decades, making it imperative that both parties acknowledge the legitimacy of each other's historical experiences and claims.

Impartial and Inclusive Mediation

To ensure a fair resolution, neutral and inclusive mediation is paramount. The international community, including influential nations and regional organisations such as the Arab League and the United Nations, must actively promote negotiations and create the conditions for a just and lasting peace. Mediators should possess a deep understanding of the historical, cultural, and political complexities involved, remaining impartial and committed to facilitating a resolution that respects the interests and welfare of both Israelis and Palestinians.

Core Issues and Guiding Principles

Addressing the core issues at the heart of the conflict is vital for a fair resolution. One of the most significant challenges is determining the borders and territorial division. Negotiations should strive for a mutually agreed-upon border that recognises the security concerns of Israel while abiding by international law and ensuring contiguity for a future Palestinian state. This can be achieved through land swaps and innovative solutions that consider the demographic realities on the ground.

The question of Jerusalem, a city considered holy by multiple faiths, requires a creative and inclusive approach. The rights of all religious communities to access and worship freely at their respective holy sites must be protected. A shared sovereignty model or internationalisation of the city's holy sites, ensuring the city remains united while allowing for the administration of different areas by Palestinians and Israelis, could be explored. This approach would require the commitment of all parties to respect each other's religious and cultural rights.

Reconciliation and Trust-Building Efforts

Any fair resolution should emphasise the importance of reconciliation and healing the wounds that have emerged from decades of conflict. Promoting people-to-people interaction, cultural exchanges, joint economic initiatives, and educational programmes can foster empathy, mutual understanding, and trust between Israelis and Palestinians. Encouraging dialogue at all levels of society, including between youth and women, can contribute to dismantling stereotypes, dispelling misconceptions, and fostering a shared vision for peaceful coexistence.

Economic Development and Prosperity

Sustainable peace requires addressing socio-economic disparities and enhancing living conditions for both Israelis and Palestinians. International assistance should be directed towards infrastructure development, job creation, sustainable agriculture, and investment in education and healthcare facilities. Initiatives that foster economic interdependence and cooperation can create incentives for peace and lay the foundations for shared prosperity. Cross-border projects that involve Israelis and Palestinians working together can promote economic cooperation and alter the dynamics on the ground.

Accountability and Transitional Justice

Accountability is crucial for building trust and ensuring a fair resolution. Alleged war crimes and human rights violations committed by either side should be thoroughly investigated, with perpetrators held accountable for their actions. Transitional justice mechanisms, such as truth commissions and reconciliation processes, can promote healing, grant reparations, and pave the way for lasting peace. Engaging with the past is not about assigning blame but rather acknowledging the suffering experienced by both Israelis and Palestinians and ensuring that justice prevails.

Political Will and Popular Support

Both domestically and internationally, sustained political will is essential for successfully implementing a fair resolution. Governments, civil society organisations, and grassroots movements must cultivate an environment conducive to dialogue, foster education about the conflict and its complexities, and advocate for peaceful coexistence. The voices of those committed to peace must be amplified, and efforts to marginalise extremist elements from both sides must be firmly reinforced. Leadership must embrace the courageous steps necessary for a fair resolution and communicate the benefits of long-lasting peace to their constituents.

Conclusion

Resolving the Israeli-Palestinian conflict is complex, requiring collective commitment and unyielding dedication. By acknowledging historical grievances, facilitating inclusive negotiations, promoting reconciliation efforts, addressing socio-economic disparities, ensuring accountability, and garnering widespread support, a fair resolution that respects the rights and aspirations of both Israelis and Palestinians is not only possible but imperative. It falls upon all of us to actively engage in a dialogue for peace, support inclusive negotiations, and strive to create a future that brings justice, security, and prosperity to both Israelis and Palestinians – a future where coexistence thrives and the wounds of the past are transformed into opportunities for growth and mutual respect. Only through genuine, sustained efforts can we pave the way for a brighter future for all those who call the region home.

CHAPTER 39

Final Thoughts on the Future of the Region

The Israeli-Palestinian conflict has been a source of pain, tragedy, and untold suffering for decades. Throughout this book, we have extensively examined the complexities, historical context, and various factors contributing to the conflict. As we conclude our exploration, we must delve even deeper into the region's future and consider an in-depth analysis of the path towards a just and lasting peace.

The future of the Israeli-Palestinian conflict remains uncertain and multifaceted, riddled with numerous challenges that must be overcome. However, it is essential to approach this uncertainty with a profound sense of hope, determination, and a steadfast commitment to justice. The first step towards a peaceful resolution is acknowledging the shared humanity and the legitimate aspirations of both Israelis and Palestinians.

A critical aspect of envisioning the future lies in recognising the psychological dimensions of the conflict. Years of violence, fear, and trauma have left deep scars on both communities. It is imperative to address the collective trauma experienced by Israelis and Palestinians, as well as the individual fractures caused by the loss of loved ones and the dislocation of families. Healing these wounds requires empathy, compassion, and an acknowledgement of the shared suffering endured by all.

To address this psychological aspect, various initiatives can be undertaken. Psycho-social support programmes can be implemented on both sides, offering counselling and therapy for individuals and communities affected by trauma. These programmes can help individuals process their emotions, heal their wounds, and foster resilience. Additionally, people-to-people interactions, such as joint projects and dialogue groups, can facilitate encounters between Israelis and Palestinians, facilitating understanding, empathy, and reconciliation.

By fostering narratives of reconciliation and understanding, it becomes possible to challenge the entrenched narratives of fear, hatred, and victimhood that perpetuate the cycle of violence. Educational systems and media outlets have a pivotal role in promoting intercultural dialogue, dispelling stereotypes, and fostering empathy amongst the younger generations, who will shape the region's future.

Curriculum reforms can incorporate inclusive and balanced narratives that highlight the shared historical, cultural, and religious heritage of both Israelis and Palestinians. These reforms would provide students with a comprehensive understanding of the other side, dispelling biases and promoting empathy. Media outlets should also prioritise objective reporting, offer platforms for diverse voices, and promote coexistence and cooperation rather than perpetuating divisiveness.

Furthermore, the future of the Israeli-Palestinian conflict also necessitates an examination of the geopolitical complexities at play. It is crucial to acknowledge the influence of regional and international actors in perpetuating or alleviating regional tensions. External powers must recognise their responsibility in fostering an environment conducive to peace, which involves refraining from actions that deepen divisions and promote violence. The international community must utilise its influence to support and strengthen diplomatic efforts while holding accountable those who perpetuate injustice and human rights violations.

Regional dynamics should also be taken into account. Engaging neighbouring countries, such as Jordan and Egypt, and other influential regional actors can contribute to building a regional framework for peace that addresses shared concerns and promotes cooperation. Regional initiatives that foster economic integration, security cooperation, and people-to-people exchanges can create an environment conducive to peace and stability.

In exploring the economic future of the region, it is essential to address the vast disparities between Israelis and Palestinians. Economic development and prosperity can serve as powerful catalysts for peace, providing incentives for stability and cooperation. The international community should invest in infrastructure, job creation, and entrepreneurship initiatives that benefit Israelis and Palestinians, bridging the economic divide and fostering interdependence. Sustainable economic growth can help address some of the root causes of the conflict while simultaneously building trust and stability.

Additionally, economic collaborations between Israelis and Palestinians have the potential to break down barriers and build mutual trust. Joint ventures, cross-border investments, and trade agreements can create interdependencies, leading to shared interests and prosperity. Examples such as the successful industrial zones in the West Bank, where Israeli and Palestinian businesses work side by side, demonstrate the potential for economic cooperation as a means of peacebuilding.

Finally, the region's future depends on the collective will of individuals, communities, governments, and the international community. It necessitates a departure from the destructive patterns of the past, with a genuine commitment to reconciliation, justice, and a vision of shared prosperity. Only through persistent efforts and robust engagement can the light of hope pierce through the darkness of despair.

Let us envision a future where Israelis and Palestinians can live in peace and thrive in an environment of mutual respect, understanding, and shared prosperity. A future where children can grow up without fear, where economic opportunities are equally accessible, and where the scars of the conflict are healed through truth, empathy, and restorative justice mechanisms.

Such a future requires significant investment in dialogue and negotiation processes that prioritise human rights, international law, and the principles of justice. It calls for an end to the occupation and the establishment of a sovereign Palestinian state alongside a secure Israel. It entails addressing the conflict's underlying grievances and root causes, such as the right of return for Palestinian refugees and the status of Jerusalem, through thoughtful and inclusive negotiations.

These negotiations should be based on internationally recognised parameters, including United Nations resolutions, previous agreements, and the Arab Peace Initiative. The United States, the European Union, and other influential actors should act as honest brokers, facilitating negotiations and providing political support. Simultaneously, regional and international organisations, such as the United Nations, should support and monitor the implementation of agreements, ensuring compliance and accountability.

In pursuing a better future for the region, let us remain vigilant in our efforts, steadfast in our beliefs, and resolute in our dedication to the fundamental values of justice and humanity. The road ahead may be arduous, but together, we can seize the opportunity for change, overcome the obstacles, and forge a path towards a future where peace prevails and the wounds of the past are finally healed.

As we draw this book close, let us remember that the Israeli-Palestinian conflict is not an intractable struggle devoid of solutions. It is a human-made problem that demands human-made solutions. By embracing the principles of justice, compassion, and empathy, we can chart a new course for the region and pave the way towards a future defined by peace, security, and dignity for all.

www.ingramcontent.com/pod-product-compliance
Lightning Source LLC
Chambersburg PA
CBHW051537020426
42333CB00016B/1978